The Space Economy

Dan Hermes and Gabe Bentz

Acknowledgements

To the space visionaries moving the world ahead at
the risk of their lives and fortunes

Acknowledgements

To the space visionaries moving the world ahead at
the risk of their lives and fortunes

Contents

Introduction

The Space Economy has been a project in the works for nearly two years and we hope will continue on for some time after this book is released.

We started "The Space Economy" blog as a way to spark discussion about coming pitfalls within the space industry that would need to be addressed, preferably sooner rather than later. Many hours went into discussion and research in order to pick topics and ideas that would be relevant. As we worked on ideas others arose and then still others until we gained a list of hundreds of topics. Some of those topics may be mentioned briefly in this book but we hope to address the rest of them in more depth in future.

As engineers we love the technology of space. But when we started out we wanted to write about not just technology but also the business, political, and social requirements for such technology to be feasible. So we took the stance of designing businesses. Each essay we wrote was a short business outline that we hoped would spark ideas in those who are better than us and have the time and resources to pursue the ideas we put forward.

Businesses were an all right direction for a period. But in order for a business to be practicable, philosophical and political considerations have to be addressed. Business may not be necessary if an area of space is communistic or something along those lines. So as time went by we began to make predictions about the overall society of space in order to validate the industries that we were describing.

As "The Space Economy" blog gained readership we realized that perhaps we should expand our audience a little. So we have published much of what was written online plus a few extras and this is what this book is.

The purpose of this book is to give the reader a perspective on where the space industry is as well as considerations on where is will go in the future.

We would like to warn the reader that there was no real organization within the blog. We simply tried to put to paper as many business, political, and technological arguments as we could in order to spark action from students and entrepreneurs who wish to enter the private space industry. So when we made this book we decided to sort the essays by a type of geographic categorization. We start with essays about space topics that directly affect or exist on Earth, then we move into orbit, then the Moon, and so on.

We hope that in our ramblings the reader is able to take away something useful. We lay claim to none of the ideas put forward in this book, if someone has a way to act upon them all the better, go for it.

Gabe Bentz and Dan Hermes

Earth

Space Board Games

The creation of tabletop/board games for the zero-gravity of space.

As space tourism and colonization begins to grow and progress the customs and pastimes of the people that spend time in space will also morph from what we know on Earth. This creates an opportunity for inventors and entrepreneurs to imagine and create things that can add to that society today.

In our digital world board games still have a strong hold of the way people spend their time. Games like chess and checkers have existed for hundreds of years. But they are all terrestrial.

In space new games can be created that function very differently from those on Earth. Space has the unique quality of no gravity. Games that were once played on a two-dimensional board can now be played in three-dimensional space.

These games will be needed. The space tourists will want every indulgence in order to make their space experience a full one. This requires activities that can only be performed in space. Space games will have to be created as resorts and cruise lines begin to be created.

And those colonists that will have a six month journey on their way to Mars or some other colony will need to have something to pass the time. A good board game is far more physically interactive and connecting than a computer game. Such games can literally help to keep crews sane on long journeys.

The design of such games can be varied. Some may simply be standard Earth games with the pieces adapted for the space environment. Something like adding magnets to keep them from floating around. Pretty easy to do

Perhaps games can be designed to have psychological benefits for the crew using them. Something along the lines of trivia games using particular images of Earth to encourage "happy thoughts" in the crew.

And of course, entirely new games can be created that are designed singularly for space. Games that may actually start in space and eventually be implemented on Earth. These create an entirely new spectrum of game design that can begin to be explored.

These little pieces of entertainment, the board game, which have been common on Earth, can easily be made common in space. It is one of those ideas that require little capital to create in an industry which is generally today.

Human Preservation Company

A company that preserves human genetics in space
One of the more exotic and maybe even "snake-oil" kinds of businesses that could be pursued in the space industry of, not only tomorrow, but today is that of selling tickets on "Preservation Spacecraft."

This is basically the idea of creating a time capsule or "stasis pod." Customers would pay to have hair, blood, or some other genetic material stored and/or preserved on a spacecraft. In this way, it could start out being marketed as either preserving the human race, should our planet be entirely wiped out, being the "ambassador" should an alien race ever find the craft, or just as a way to satisfy personal ego.

Now, this is a bit of an outlandish idea, but not unheard of. Many people have a desire to be preserved in some way. What better place to preserve something than in the nothingness of space? Many people also believe that the entire human race should have a few ways to mark our existence to extraterrestrials should we ever destroy ourselves. These are both legitimate reasons for some people to pay to have their genetic material sent to space.

As far as the technical aspects are concerned. A beginning company could simply create small satellites, such as CubeSats, which are outfitted to protect genetic materials from the radiation of space. This is a relatively simple thing to accomplish. The spacecraft itself would probably need some type of transmitter that can last for longer periods of time. This would be to cater to those that want to leave something for E.T. so the green men can find and recognize the capsule as from a technological society.

Where would these spacecraft be sent? Well, just starting out they could be sent into high Earth orbit. This would keep them in space for around a hundred years. As technology grows, these craft could begin to be sent out of the solar system like space probes have just begun to accomplish (Voyager). This expansion would be marketed as the "seeding of the universe" by humans. The company would be able to profess how the genetic material may start the advent of life on other worlds and the people that purchase the ticket for their DNA would be the "parents" of that life. (think Prometheus)

Understandably this business can be twisted, very easily, into some kind of fraud. Having people buy space for blood samples on a CubeSat that is sent into space and then burns back to Earth and no one would ever know. Or the genetic material could be launched and not appropriately protected so that it is obliterated by the cold and radiation of space. But if approached correctly this "preservation craft" does have a legitimate mission to many people. (it all depends on who you are)

Far in the future, should a company like this exist, its purpose most likely would be some type of "whole body" preservation. It would be a model like the cryonics companies of today, preserve entire humans for revival at a later date, either by humans or E.T.

There is no telling how profitable a business like this would be. It is has never been tried, though such things have been performed for free on some launches, for dignitaries. But whether it is a complete business or not, is still unclear. Perhaps it is an idea that companies, or even researchers, can adopt to help pay the large cost of space launches today. A little blood or hair is not a heavy thing to add to a spacecraft, but it may be worth several thousand dollars to the customer that wishes to purchase a place for their DNA in a launch. (this actually creates another opportunity to create the protective containers for the material by yet another company, but we'll leave that to the reader to consider.)

Human preservation is something many people think about today. While we can't explore space completely yet, it is possible to send ourselves out into it and create a "human backup." This ideal is something that many people can relate to and creates a unique opportunity that can be explored immediately. From someone as low as a college student to as high as an experienced business magnate this concept can be pursued.

Astronaut Camps

Live a week like an astronaut.

A company that puts people through rigorous astronaut training and simulations. This business can be approached from both the experiential entertainment/learning side or the serious launch preparation side.

This business could begin as space camp on steroids. Just like when some people take nature survival classes or mock SEAL training, this "camp" could create the experience of training for and being an astronaut. People could go through zero-g flights, centrifuges, and all kinds of tough workouts. Then, after a time of "training" they would be able to be put into the simulation of their choice. Perhaps "repair" a space station mock-up in the swimming pool, or visit the "Mars Colony" on campus.

Of course, it doesn't have to take such an extreme direction. Creation of the experiences of being on Mars or the Moon for a week as if one were a real astronaut (an extreme space VR) could also be a viable business model on the entertainment side.

Such a camp could also become the industry contractor for preparing prospective space tourists and explorers for their launches and missions. It would be in charge of training and certification of most space passengers in the weeks prior to their flights. Currently, this is performed by the launch company. Being able to outsource passenger preparation would allow those companies to focus on their primary business of engineering vehicles.

Space Camps and "learning to be an astronaut" has been around for a while. And companies like Zero-G are capitalizing on people wanting to have a space experience. The problem is that space camps have been relatively superficial and don't capitalize on the complete experience. And Zero-G is focusing only on the weightless flights. A true astronaut camp would need to go deeper into the experience and leverage all connections with companies like Zero-G and others like it that will emerge.

Now there is always the danger that the entertainment or learning aspect of the camp will not get the response needed to maintain it. It will have a marketing and presentation problem. After all, space doesn't quite have the attraction that it did in the 1950's-1970's. But if that should fail initially, the entertainment concept could be kept in reserve for when space opens up again and public interest is in that direction. Until then, contracts for actual training for missions would be adequate and increasing as more launch vehicles begin operations and human traffic increases.

This kind of a business has a lot of facets. Practical, leisure, extreme sports, team-building. An "Astronaut Camp" could take any kind of form or focus. If it is to cater to the general public it would have to be something fun and exciting that isn't too harsh but still give the real feel for space. But if it wants to be a part of the actual private space industry, in a big way, it will need to eventually become what some of Nasa's manned spaceflight centers are.

But overall, the idea of an all-in "Astronaut Camp" is something that can be approached today and, with proper execution, could be viable independently of the current space industry.

Spacesuit Maker

If anyone wants to do anything in any part of space personally, they have to have a spacesuit. But with each new environment a different spacesuit is required. There are suits for when a rocket launches, for when someone takes a spacewalk, for the Moon, for Mars. As the industry grows the variety of suits will have to also. Specialty suits will need to be created for orbital construction workers and extra-comfortable suits for tourists. And all of these people will always need the suits and new environments will need new suits. The market will always exist and will always be growing. Just like the clothing market on Earth now. A few companies have already started work on the spacesuits that will define the new industry. But there is plenty of room for talented individuals with a will to help people operate in space.

Spacesuits have been the domain of NASA for many years. And though there have been significant developments, spacesuits are extremely poor in design. The number one reason is because they are so arduous to use. They are like having an inflated bag around you that you must push and pull against for even the smallest movement. Even fit astronauts get a workout during a spacewalk. This is not something that would be ideal for a space tourist. But there are solutions to this problem and others that exist. Many have been researched and are in the public domain. And there are always new solutions to old problems.

Spacesuits are also not very sexy. The suits used by astronauts on the ISS today make you think of a marshmallow man with a helmet. But the current space industry is all about hype and image. It must convey a message of advanced technology and appear as one would imagine from seeing Sci-Fi movies. If the industry doesn't do this then it looks like "the same old thing." What better way to inspire people and get them behind you than to show them groups of people in futuristic spacesuits? For this reason spacesuit manufacturers have to make their suits awesome. (SpaceX actually stipulated to their spacesuit contractor that the suits look "badass")

But on the practical side, spacesuits are really just small spaceships. This could be a design approach in the future when suits need to be created in bulk quantities to "get the job done." Instead of working to create a suit with flexible arms and legs, a company could just make a can with arms. This is actually what the early space pioneers imagined. Such a "suit" could be used by construction crews for building space stations. Or even as a disposable unit.

What about when we go back to the Moon or even Mars. While some of the suits of the time may be modified for the terrestrial environments there will be a need for different kinds of suits in each case. Suits will have to deal with the stress of dirt and grime which is absent in the void as well as the differences in atmosphere, gravity, and activities.

Overall, spacesuits are something with a lot of design leeway allowed, a lot of design improvements needed, and a lot of niche variations required. That makes it into a very clear market opportunity. Not to mention the fact that few launch companies want to have the responsibility of creating their own spacesuits. Such side projects take away from companys', like SpaceX, primary mission of developing launch vehicles.

Orbital Outfitters and Final Frontier Design are a couple of the companies that are already working to create spacesuits for the new private space industry. Wisely, they are not only focusing on creating spacesuits that are functionally better than any suit that has been created before, but also on giving them the futuristic look that space tourists and the world will want to see. Orbital has been contracted by SpaceX and XCOR to develop pressure suits for their vehicle crews and Final Frontier recently completed a successful Kickstarter campaign.

The space industry needs spacesuits, everywhere and for everything. Construction, play, escape, appearance, planetary exploration. These many applications require many different kinds of suits.

A spacesuit company is not a particularly expensive or technically challenging company to begin. Final Frontier began with a fashion designer and an ex-spacesuit designer. Such a company can gain a foothold by making pressure suits now but would have unlimited expansion possibilities as its competence grows. And even though Orbital Outfitters and Final Frontier Design already have a head start, their solutions are not perfect. A clever designer and/or entrepreneur can improve on the spacesuit as it is viewed right now and become the source for creating a very necessary piece of equipment that the entire industry has and always will need.

Astronaut Recruiter

An organization for the selection and recruiting of astronauts.

Astronauts have long held one of the most selective jobs in the world. They are the best of the best. But finding people that are able to live up to the expectations of the position is very difficult, and changing.

When humans were just beginning to go to space nearly all of the astronauts were chosen for their physical abilities and their skill with aircraft. Space and the vehicles to get there were such unknowns the astronauts were supposed to be able to deal with whatever was thrown at them. With the creation of space stations, astronauts changed to more the scientist than the test pilot. They perform space research without as many of the risks and unknowns that early astronauts faced.

Astronauts are continuing to change. Individual psychologies and skills are going to need to be mixed and matched depending upon missions. Like the equipment sent on a spaceship for a mission, the crews will need to be tailored for the task.

The typical means of selecting astronauts in the past has been to go through a process of applications, interviews, tests and evaluations. NASA can take over a year selecting new potential candidates. But, with human space missions on the rise and colonization in the future, the long arduous methods of choosing astronauts will not continue to be feasible. When space missions occur on a regular basis it is just not practical to spend a year finding the perfect crew or drawing from a pool of perfect astronauts.

For example, Mars One is working to put together a crew for a one way mission to Mars. This crew will have to take care of itself. It can't be only engineers, or scientists, or doctors, or even one single gender. The crew must also be able to live with each other inside of a tin can for months or even years. They must be perfectly cohesive and comprehensively skilled for this particular adventure or it could all end in disaster.

Mars One screened 200,000 applications over a period of several months. The selection of astronauts should not require such long selection periods. Imagine if Mars One hadn't needed to create and control the entire process itself but was able to talk to an Astronaut Recruiter who could pull together the perfect team for their space mission just as one would for a football team or company.

This organization would essentially be an astronaut Linked-In. A company that is constantly looking for, sorting, and selecting talent and personalities that can be combined to create the perfect space crew for a particular mission.

Such a company would likely begin life as something as simple as a website. Aspiring astronauts could complete a profile which would include information about accomplishments, physical characteristics and even basic psychological evaluations and other tests. Then companies that are looking to create a crew for some type of mission will be able to access that site in order to search in a semi-sorted pool of choices.

As the company grows it could continually develop its means of evaluating potential astronauts. Incorporating algorithms along the lines of dating sites for the creation of potential teams. Sorting people into groups based on skills and personal preferences.

Eventually the company could integrate face to face interviews and recruiting. Becoming the HR resource for the space industry. Such evolution would allow the company to be the "go to" sub-contractor of spacefarers. Then, instead of someone, like Mars One, having to accept 200,000 applications it could simply call up the Astronaut Recruiter, give them mission specs then a recommendation of persons would be sent in return for a fee.

The "secret sauce" of an Astronaut Recruiter would be how it is able to evaluate potential crews psychologically and physically. For this reason the founders of such a company would likely be ex-psychologist or HR personnel that have learned how to tell when one person will fit a position or situation and another would not.

The revenue model for such a company would be two sided. Just as Linked-In charges members for a premium account an Astronaut Recruiter could charge potential applicants for increased access to particular resources. The Astronaut Recruiter could also charge prospective employers for the search service rendered as with any employee search site or organization.

Currently, the market is not in dire need of a recruiter for astronauts. Though if it had existed two years ago it could have been a part of the Mars One search.

However, in coming years crews will increasingly need to be tailored. The men and women needed to go mine the Moon, work in orbit, or colonize Mars will all have to have very different combinations of characteristics, just as in any job. The need for someone who can construct a perfect space team will become very great and is something which can be begun today.

Space Food

A company for the manufacture and distribution of space foodstuffs.

Within the next ten years a permanent commercial human population will be established in orbit and beyond. But how will these people be supported. An entire industry based upon the needs of these space residents and tourists will need to be created.

Food will be the most difficult consumable to supply to these space communities. People can live with stale air and recycled water but food has to be an experience filled with flavor as well as nutrition. But creating something that meets those two criteria while, ideally, having a shelf life of months, without refrigeration, is a tall order. In the old days salted pork with an occasional orange was considered a complete meal, our more civilized society must create something better for our explorers.

Food in space has been a challenge that even NASA has not met yet. While they have learned to freeze, vacuum seal, irradiate, and store food so that much of it will not spoil on a long trip, and even still have some flavor, there are some foods which we take for granted on Earth that are considered delicacies in orbit because they simply can't be prepared or obtained in space. Baking bread is a challenge which isn't completely solved.

All the deficiencies in the cuisine of the Void are opportunities. Food is something that is easily redesigned and adapted while also having infinite possibilities and potential. And the best part is the products are needed today and not only in space but right here at home.

Many facets of the space food industry exist. The potential for space gardens and specific tools for accomplishing the kind of culinary feats that are possible on Earth are all applicable, but for the purposes of this essay we will focus on the opportunity of providing prepackaged food that is meant to be a meal "practically" ready to eat in orbit.

Here in the early days of the space industry which is heavily focused on tourism and government contracts the food will have to be of a special kind of hybrid. It will have to provide a pleasurable experience that is unique to space but also contain the nutrition to allow someone to live off of it. This will require that a space food manufacturer create an initial product that is almost nostalgic, the kind of freeze dried and in a toothpaste tube that tourists would expect on a trip so that they can feel like their image of astronauts. But this paste would still be something that someone who isn't just in space to visit can live off of.

In order to cut on costs it would likely be something along the lines of a paste or solid bar that can be shaped and formed into whatever the customer needs. So just like ice cream, where you can use vanilla as a base for chocolate or strawberry, this Space Paste would contain all the nutrition a person needs but could be flavored and shaped into whatever the customer wants. Soylent is a current product that very nearly meets this criterion.

Such a product would also need to deal with yet another problem brought on by space food, boredom. How many people can say that they love to eat oatmeal morning noon and night? Food is something that adds excitement and interest to our lives. A space food that can be practical, in that is can be packed, stored, and provide nutrition, but also fills the human need for change and diversity in flavor, is exactly what is needed today.

Fortunately, unlike so much of the space industry, the technology and products developed for space food will not trickle down to be used in the Earth food industry as so many space developments are claimed to do. It would, instead, be immediately and directly marketable without having to redesign any part of it. Imagine extremely dense nutritional supplements that are able to be packed and stored for years while remaining light weight. Such products could be loaded into disaster relief trucks or into hiking backpacks. Any company that produces such wears would not have to depend solely upon the space industry to sustain itself.

The competition in space food will be fierce. While food designed for space is applicable on Earth, the reverse is also true to some extent. After all it would not take a great deal of effort for brand name protein bars and supplements to be customized for space. And the infinite variation of food doesn't allow for much protection through intellectual property. But a small start-up can certainly gain ground by moving now and gaining contracts with the rising private launch companies, with paying customers who want their space peanuts during the flight.

A company dedicated to space food would be something that would certainly be able to diversify. While an initial product would want to be a catch-all design, all further developments could range from old style toothpaste tubes of peanut butter to the creation of the most advanced recipes and cooking equipment anyone has ever seen. Really, the creation of food in space is one of the most difficult pieces of chemistry that anyone has ever had to undertake.

The market for space food has existed for some time. Space museums and other tourist traps have long provided freeze dried cuisine just like the astronauts used to make. In the actual industry the government space agencies have been the only providers of TV dinners fit for the space station. This won't continue to be sufficient. Human traffic is only going to increase and NASA is continuing to lose their budget and is not prepared for food production in large quantities. Just as new launch vehicle providers need someone to make spacesuits they need someone to cook meals. It can and needs to be done today, and even if it means freeze drying your favorite smoothie blend, it would be better than what the industry has available now.

Ecological Benefits of Space Mining

We are continually working to explain the benefits of space commercialization. One that has been overlooked by the industry has been the ecological benefits of using resources from space. This pertains particularly to the mining industry.

Mining has a notable ecological impact on our planet. Mountains are literally removed every year in order to supply the raw materials needed for our increasingly industrialized planet. But this may not be a sustainable or necessary practice. Space mining would be capable of replacing it and without negative ecological impact.

Asteroids are rocks out of the ground already floating in space. Excavating them has no negative impact on our solar system, as long as it is not done in orbit. Millions of times more material, than what we dig on Earth, is available in our solar system, which can be exploited, with proper infrastructure. And this infrastructure is growing ever closer.

Many space advocates sell it as something which is the future of our race as a means of survival from cataclysmic asteroid strikes and the like or as a means to satisfy the human need to explore. While these reasons are founded, they do not resound with some parts of the population on Earth. Space has to provide some benefit other than simply making money, exploring, and preventing destruction. Space must create a more encompassing return for Earth to be worth it. Ecology is one such return. The fact that the commercialization of space will help to solve ecological problems on Earth is a grand reason to work toward space.

Now, certainly many will argue that space mining will still have negative effects on earthen ecosystems. Because dirty rockets must be launched and rocks dropped from the sky.

This view has little credence as it assumes that rocket technology will remain as it is, which it won't, and that the asteroids would have to be delivered as raw materials to the surface of the Earth, which they won't. Space mining will revolve around the refining and manufacturing of materials in orbit (or possibly on the Moon) which can then be delivered to Earth with a gliding space plane. And rockets are already powered by combinations of hydrogen and oxygen which combine to create...water. In fact, the kerosene burning Falcon 9 is "cleaner" than the solid rocket boosters of the space shuttle so we are already creating a greener space industry.

Mining companies would do well to explore space mining as a part of their future. Not only are the resources abundant, but the good will that it would generate by "working to preserve Earth ecosystems" would be valuable to such a company. And along the road space technologies developed could be applied to Earth problems. Caterpillar, which makes mining machinery, apparently sees this potential as it is partnering with NASA to develop space mining technologies.

Space Toys

A company for the creation of toys uniquely suited for the environment of space.

While the beauty of space is awe inspiring, when you live there for long periods of time it starts to lose its charm. Diversions for space travelers will have to become an industry. Toys and games will need to be created which tourists and explorers can enjoy while locked inside of a can or bubble.

So what would a space toy look like? Well, the simplest is a ball. Astronauts in the ISS have used balls as entertainment in the zero-g environment for years. While entertaining, space-ball will lose its novelty, especially to people who are watching it. And in an industry where public opinion will have huge sway, it is important to create a "Space Experience" that can't be replicated. Catch in space is still just catch.

So any kind of space toy must be able to exist only in space, otherwise the romance and desire is gone from those who are not a part of it.

So, what can occur in a weightless environment that can't anywhere else. The first thing is structures. Gossamer creations can exist in space that would collapse on Earth. A building set made of straws could be an option. Or perhaps a strategy game, such as dominoes, where players attempt to limit the movies of other players. Perhaps a dynamic game where players set certain pieces in motion without disrupting others. Or maybe instead of using a board, each space is a separate piece that floats in midair. Anything that utilizes the 3-D, floating experience of space.

Now, in the current space environment of high launch costs and no-frills design, a toy may not be high on the shopping list. This is founded. Given the choice between a toy and a tool many will choose the tool when going to space. The weight of even a few pounds of toys or games costs thousands of dollars to launch.

Fortunately, it is no longer necessary to launch toys. They can be beamed to orbit. Made-In-Space recently sent a 3-D printer to the ISS that has been making plastic tools and spare parts for several months. It would be so simple to just e-mail a set of space Legos.

3-D printing will allow crews of space missions to not only create necessary parts and tools but also a little entertainment with no launch cost. And when the toy becomes boring it can be melted down and turned into something else.

Because of technologies like 3-D printing, space toys are something that can be created today. A high school kid with Google Sketch-up could create something that could be sold to the astronauts on the ISS tomorrow.

Space toys will be a low-cost-of-entry business. And, at this point, there is no competition because no one has really considered it. But it will be an industry as tourism heats up in coming years. Plus explorers on long missions to Mars will love to have an inventory of "made for space" entertainment that they can download when they want it, play with it, and then turn into a spare part.

Anyone with some time and creativity can create a business that would never have to have inventory, but would help to support the psychological wellness of many space missions in the future. Maybe by just creating a 3-D printable space chess set.

Space Movie

How often have great designers, engineers, and scientists been interviewed, and when asked about their original inspiration they reference some movie or show.

Star Wars, Star Trek, 2001: A Space Odyssey, Buck Rogers, The Jetsons. These movies and TV shows have literally inspired thousands of people to make the fiction fact.

Now, within the last ten years, point to a movie or TV show which could be the definitive media trigger to inspire new technologists. Many will respond with Interstellar, Avatar, Star Wars, and Star Trek. But the trouble is, of those answers, only Interstellar and Avatar were really new concepts. But across the board, none of these movies had at their core the wonder of discovery or space travel itself. Interstellar was not about exploration but about a man separated from his family. Avatar was not about exploration but the dangers and warnings of what may come from it.

In the last decade there has been no single movie which has defined the glory and wonder of space exploration and expansion. In the movies where this has been a possibility, Space has simply been a backdrop, not the focus.

How can an industry which requires a level of public opinion and knowledge to survive, by driving tourism ambitions and potentially tax dollars, survive without becoming a part of culture.

Movies and media really define the state of American society at any given time. People lived and breathed space exploration, when the moon landings were happening. Today, the attempt to land a rocket on a barge to reduce spaceflight costs by factors of 10, barely makes it onto Google News.

A movie needs to be made about space travel and exploration. A movie which actually captures the imagination and hope of the world. A movie which makes people "starry-eyed" about space travel again.

While we at "The Space Economy" are not fiction writers, what story could be more endearing than one set ten years from now when the space industry is fully active? Every space movie in recent years, or ever, has begun 50-100 years in the future. People will be amazed and excited by a date at the beginning of a movie of just 5-10 years in the future.

Note: Since this section was written "The Martian," the novel by Andy Weir was turned into a movie. And while it has not been released at the time of this book's publication, it does have make space, exploration, and survival as the focus.

Space Burial

One of the more interesting space businesses, which is really as old as spaceflight itself, is the idea of space burials.

As a means of disposing of the deceased space burials are actually quite practical and even more emotional. Leaving someone in a place where they will perpetually drift and travel and perhaps even seed life into arid worlds, is a very romantic way to send them on to the next life.

Space burials have been going on since the very first moon landers. Ashes of people have been sent up ever since. Celestis, Inc is a company that has formed around the idea of space burial. Celestis purchases empty space on launches and fills them with samples of cremated remains. The people that have been buried in space include Gene Roddenberry, the creator of Star Trek, as well as several hundred other people.

However, at this point a typical space burial includes less than an ounce of ashes in a sample tube which take the ride, but then typically come back down as the orbit decays or the mission ends. Very few people have had remains placed permanently into space. And certainly, there have been no full bodies sent, only cremated remains.

Space burials as a business, are actually very simple. A basic set of vials are made and ashes inserted. Then they are placed in an empty corner of the next possible launch. Low weight, low effort, but a very moving way to be buried.

In future, space burials will no doubt become much more commonplace. While they are currently reserved for the rich and famous, as launches become ever more frequent so will the space to place the small caskets. Someday entire bodies may be buried in space. Though there will no doubt be restrictions on this practice to ensure that tourists in orbit are not surprised by a cadaver outside of the station.

Space burials will also grow to be much more than a typical burial. They may come to epitomize the ideals of space travel. Imagine an astronaut or scientist dedicating their entire life to space but dying before their dream was realized. Perhaps they wanted to reach an asteroid or set foot on Mars. Sending their remains to those places fulfills and legitimizes their life's work and can inspire others to follow.

Space burials are likely one of the oldest commercial space businesses and will likely remain after many others die. While at this moment they may seem a bit sterile compared to a casket and flowers, they are far more meaningful and beautiful. Space is an eternity, why not place a person's remains in eternity after they have entered it.

Earth Orbit

Orbital Power Generation

Electricity is the driving force of the modern world. It powers our homes, our devices. It controls traffic and heat. For many, being without electricity would be equivalent to being without the sun each day. And this need will only continue to grow.

Electric vehicles will become more prevalent and possibly even replace gas engines. The world population is growing, with it the demand for electricity in houses and devices. Not to mention the fact that one-quarter of the world is currently without electricity and will eventually have it. Even without that growth, demand for electricity today is more than the supply. New means of power generation must be created.

As science progresses nuclear power plants may be able to move toward fusion instead of fission. This would create a great amount of power and would most likely meet the demand. But at this point that is not a viable option or even near to becoming one.

Renewables also have room for improvement. But no matter how efficient solar or wind become they will simply occupy too much space and continue to be an eyesore. Their physical footprint is too large to meet future demand.

Here is the opportunity for space. There is plenty of space up in space. Anything in orbit around the Earth is invisible to the naked eye. We also have an unobstructed view of a giant fusion reactor at the center of our solar system, the Sun. Orbital solar power is a proven technology and is potentially a huge source of electrical power.

The reason solar power is so inefficient on Earth is due to two problems. The atmosphere and engineering limitations.

The atmosphere absorbs a 30 percent of solar energy before it ever reaches the ground on a clear day, not to mention night-time and when there is heavy cloud cover. This is not a problem in orbit because there is no atmosphere. And while there would still be day and night, they are not equal. An orbiting station can remain in sunlight for 99 percent of an orbit.

From the engineering standpoint, solar cells are only around 10-15 percent efficient today. However, unlike something like fusion, the performance of solar cells is increasing yearly. But there is no requirement to use solar cells either. An orbital station could just be a large mirror that focuses the Sun's energy onto a steam turbine in the station.

There is only one problem with a solar orbital station. How does the power get from orbit to the ground? It would have to be through wireless transmission. This could be done through microwaves or lasers. Both are proven technologies. However they require receiver stations on the ground. While these stations would have to be of a size comparable to a standard solar station today, they would be fewer in number.

With the wireless power transmission there is liability involved. If the transmission beam strays from the receiver station, it could potentially cause damage to nearby areas. But this is simple to control and the worst damage that has been predicted is sunburns a little more quickly.

The initial cost of the station, with current infrastructure, is too great to substantiate the construction of it. Studies performed by SERT (Space Solar Power Exploratory Research and Technology Group) found that launch costs would have to be as low as $100-$200 per pound to make the concept financially feasible. Current launch costs are at best $1,000 a pound. But with the development of reusable vehicles that price will drop to the range required.

The orbital construction costs would also be something to consider. Anyone working to create an orbital power station would want to have a very clear construction infrastructure in place. This could be robots or even a dedicated manned space construction station. Neither of these exists today.

But if the power station were designed along the lines of an inflatable that could be assembled with very few pieces the infrastructure would not be nearly as necessary.

At this moment all of the technology for an orbital solar power station exists and is proven. The trouble is that the infrastructure to build it is not in place. This is changing rapidly, but resources for such a project will not be complete enough for at least another ten years. But at that point, the demand for electricity will have risen to such a degree that orbital stations will likely be a necessity and a large business opportunity.

Space Utility Company

Electricity is absolutely necessary for any and all space stations and space vehicles. Electricity warms or cools the interior, it creates drinkable water, and it even propels some craft. Modern spacecraft have to carry some means of power generation with them if they are meant to remain in space for any extended period of time. This is usually a set of solar panels and a bank of batteries. But these power generation systems add extra weight to the launch of these systems as well as the extra expense to design and integrate the system for each spacecraft. But this can all be avoided. Smaller versions of the "Orbital Solar Power Station" could be created as a means to power spacecraft. This would eliminate the need for each craft to have its own power generation system.

A space power station would essentially be a small solar plant. A group of solar panels or a mirror and turbine. But it would be outfitted with a wireless power transmitter, perhaps microwave or laser based. With this station in place, other spacecraft could simply be fitted with a receiver and then be placed near the power station in order to be given the power they need. This would reduce the amount of weight that the ship or station needs to have hauled into orbit and would reduce the design effort of making the ship completely self-sufficient.

The power station would essentially become an orbital utility company providing power to anyone that wishes to be included in its "grid." It would be able to charge the companies/nations that own the powered spacecraft and would be able to grow with demand simply by adding either more stations or increasing the size of existing ones.

Orbital power stations for other spacecraft are a very viable business at this moment. Every spacecraft that is being designed is trying to cut weight. The elimination of a set of solar panels would be a huge step forward for the industry. Such a power station would not even be expensive to create. Some development of the beaming technology would be required, but the cost of launch and construction would be relatively small. Such a station could be sent into orbit with a single SpaceX Falcon Heavy launch, around 56 million dollars, cheap by space standards.

The dangers of this concept are that the station would never be allowed to have a power outage. A blackout could make millions of people become lost, if powering GPS satellites, or even kill someone, if powering a manned space station. But this can be avoided by simply creating a network of the stations to provide the appropriate redundancy.

The economics of this kind of a system have not been completely worked out. Whether it is a viable business model to replace individual solar systems with a single power station is numerically unknown. But if implemented properly, the ability to allow companies to save money in the short term by paying for less development and lower launching costs, will certainly attract many players in the space industry who launch satellites.

Overall, space power stations are something that would be a relatively cheap space business to get into tomorrow, if the industry accepts it. It is something that can start small and grow organically,

with the industry that has to have electrical power
no matter what.

Orbital Construction Yard

    As the cost to launch materials into space
decreases, larger and more complex structures will
begin to be assembled around Earth. The construction
of these space stations and ships will become a
process far more involved than simply plugging a few
capsules together. With complexity increasing, the
cost of the construction will increase as individual
companies create their own infrastructure to build
these space stations. But that doesn't have to be
the case. If there was a single construction
organization or shipyard in space, populated with
the necessary personnel and equipment needed to
assemble and then place spacecraft, it would reduce
the cost and the preparation required for the owners
of the spacecraft.

    The creation of a construction site in orbit
would become the basis for all future space
manufacturing. Imagine a potential application just
ten years away. Bigelow Aerospace will most likely
be starting to create space hotels from its
inflatable space modules. But as it stands now, each
capsule will have to be launched and positioned
independently. This means the space station will
become something along the lines of the ISS today, a
central spine with modules attached to it. This is
because more complex configurations aren't possible
with current construction techniques. For example if
the Bigelow modules were to be constructed as a
ring, in order to create an artificial gravity spin,
it would be a much more complex assembly operation
than using the traditional design and may not even
be possible in some instances.

    An orbital construction yard could solve all of
those problems because it would be a single place to
send all pieces of a project without having to
consider the complex construction, because the

construction site would handle all of that. The construction station could create complex configurations because it would have the aid of robotic arms, and number of tools, and multiple workers, allowing them to place pieces very easily and in a controlled environment. Then, once constructed, each spacecraft could be deployed to its ideal location, making room for the next project.

But this kind of construction yard wouldn't even have to be just for construction. It could be in charge of the refurbishment of outdated equipment and the scavenging of ruined space craft. In this way it could become the trading post of used space parts and the single resource for keeping the growing number of satellites in good repair.

Going that far would require the station to keep a few small ships around that are capable of retrieving objects in need of repair. But the creation of robotic versions of that type of "Space Tug" is already underway by organizations like DARPA, the Chinese, and even the Swiss.

Now the concept is sound but what would be the technical implementation? An initial station would essentially be a set of crew quarters and some basic equipment like Canadarms to perform the collection and orbital assembly of satellites. It could almost be a permanent Space Shuttle in orbit, something that can move freely in orbit in order to repair and assemble new systems. Then as the demand and the size of projects grow, the station could go from being mobile to being in a permanent location that companies bring the pieces to have them assembled. This station would be something very similar to what people see in Star Trek shows. A large cage to contain floating parts and a series of robotic arms to position items as the crew assembles it.

The crews of these construction stations will be the most vital component. While they will be assisted robotically, human labor will always be necessary. These crews will be on par with the top astronauts today. Engineers with a fortitude to

38

accomplish incredibly complex tasks alone in orbit. They will be familiar with all the current assembly techniques and will need to learn new ones just as construction workers on Earth today.

The station most likely will not be able to support any kind of complex systems, like gravity simulation through rotation. Such systems would interfere with the work that must be done. These early stations will remain very much like current technology. A few modules for the crew to float through and very basic rations. But the conditions will be able to improve over time. As new projects come into the construction site the crew of the station will be well supplied, since any extra space on the launch vehicles could be dedicated to fresh amenities for the crew. And with that traffic there will undoubtedly be many opportunities to rotate the crew every few months. Overall the conditions will be nearly identical to that of the International Space Station (ISS) today, but with the potential of continual improvement

The business structure of such a station could be highly flexible. The company that creates these stations could deploy them and then sell them, like a house, to space companies wishing to perform their own construction in space. This would mean that the development and construction of the station itself would be all that is required, but the outfitting and manpower would be handled by the client. The other option is to completely own the station and lease construction and repair services to other companies and governments. This system requires much more infrastructure, such as robotic carriers and crews, to be handled by the station company. But, in the early stages this may be ideal to allow for more streams of revenue.

Any idea of creating an orbital construction site would be an incredibly expensive proposition. But the costs could be mitigated because the concept doesn't require a whole new system to be put in place. The station can function perfectly with the existing architectures in use, requiring little to no R&D. When the ISS comes up for retirement, it could even be retrofitted as such a station. Adding a few more Canadarms, a construction cage, and a vehicle for moving finished structures to their locations in orbit could make it perform quite well. Construction systems could even be piggy-backed off of future space hotels.

Overall, an orbital construction yard is simply a better means of creating, deploying, and maintaining space structures. Having a central location that has all the resources needed to assemble such projects would aid the industry greatly. Stations would no longer have to be designed to plug together one module at a time, certain spacecraft would be able to have new life breathed into them, and the construction yard might even become the centralized point of quality spacecraft parts from deconstructed spacecraft, things very valuable to future space explorers.

Mobile Space Power Plants

The Orbital Power Station (OPS) was a concept for providing large amounts of clean energy to Earth. However, what if it could also be used elsewhere? As colonies begin to be created on the Moon and even Mars they will need some source of power. What if a mobile power station (MPS) could be created to provide energy to these colonies?

The traditional plans for creating colonies (we'll focus on the Moon) have been to send all of the required equipment to the surface of the Moon and set it up there. But the trouble with this concept is that the location of the people is rarely the ideal location for the solar power station and vice-versa. On the Moon people will need to set up base in the walls of craters in order to be protected from meteors and radiation, but solar plants must be completely exposed. The extra labor of building an entire solar array separate from the base adds a great deal of cost and effort to an already difficult endeavor.

Having the solar plant placed on the surface also creates the issue of night and day. Large battery banks will need to be installed to power the moon base at night. This adds weight to be shipped and more reliance on a system that can break down. The entire system of a terrestrial solar power plant is faulty and complex. The transport and the construction simply are too difficult.

But all of this can be avoided if 1-2 solar power plants were placed in orbit above the base. These plants would be able to provide continuous power to the base by beaming energy to the surface using microwaves or lasers. (All this is explained in "Orbital Power Station") And since they would not have to land on the surface or even be on the same ship, landing craft would not have to carry as much fuel, reducing the cost of the mission. The only thing that would need to be installed on the surface would be a receiving array to gather the energy beamed by the power stations and this is much simpler than installing solar panels.

Power stations such as these would be relatively simple to create, especially if they are already in use around the Earth. They could simply be a rigid array of solar panels with an ion engine attached. Ion engines along the lines of VASMIR would be ideal for this application. Unlike most ships, the MPS would be able to provide the power needed for a high thrust ion engine since power generation is its only job. Making the cost of transport extremely cheap since little to no fuel is needed.

The one final advantage of an MPS is its continual mobility. If a base is finally outfitted with a reactor that provides the required power, then the MPS is able to move on to the next spot that needs it. In this sense it can have a very long operational lifetime. In addition, it wouldn't even have to move to another base. An MPS could function as a temporary power source for space stations under construction all around Earth or even as a backup for faulty satellites. Keeping the lights on until their permanent power supplies come along.

The overall construction and technology of the MPS is proven already. The only development required would be in the energy beaming technology. But an early version, which simply serves as a stand-in in Earth orbit, wouldn't need that. It could be physically plugged into the customer spacecraft.

Because of its long life cycle and mobility any company to create an MPS would want to take the strategy of a standard utility. Charging by the amount of energy provided over a section of time. The return on investment would be slow, but since the MPS could move from one job to another it would almost never be out of work.

This is a very basic idea that does have a place in the future and current space industry. It may begin as a small power source for capsules on their way to the ISS and then move on to powering temporary science satellites until their orbit decays. These menial jobs will prove its viability for when the moon and Mars bases begin to be created.

A Company for Reactivating Vintage Spacecraft

There are more spacecraft added to the menagerie in orbit every year. Some are operational. Many are not. But that is not because they are broken.

Many spacecraft simply have served their purpose. They are no longer needed or have become out of date. So they are shut down.

This collection of used satellites and probes (basically space junk) leaves an opportunity for entrepreneurs to repurpose them by simply regaining contact with them, creating new missions, and perhaps maintaining the vintage equipment needed to operate them.

The chance here is that the all of the expensive work of designing and launching the craft has already been done by someone else and now the scavenger gets all of that for free, outdated though it may be. All a new company would have to do is design new missions for the craft and recreate the tools needed to operate it. This just takes a few software or electrical engineers

Now a satellite that used to monitor Earth weather until its resolution became too poor, can instead become an open source orbital photography platform. Or it could be moved into a new orbit to be used as a practice dummy for docking. Or in the case of the ISEE-3 Reboot Project, it can be sent to study an asteroid.

The ISEE-3 Reboot Project, at the time of this writing, was a crowdfunding effort underway to perform the kind of spacecraft refurbishment just discussed. The group wishes to regain contact with a a defunct solar probe and command it to fire its engines so that is can be sent to explore a nearby asteroid. While they are doing this simply as an exercise and valiant research effort, the results from the project could be the foundation of a future space company.

The company that pursues this kind of a mission would basically just be the antique dealer of spacecraft. You go to their shop and you find the cathode tube box TV of spacecraft and buy control of it to drop an anvil onto it.

And this company doesn't have to make the old satellites do anything complex. The regaining of a means of controlling them is of huge value. With that returned control, the space junk can be collected, repurposed, reused, scrapped, or eliminated. All necessary operations in the space industry are gaining a litter problem.

Any company that regains control of defunct spacecraft would have a large foothold in the private space industry as it becomes the dealer of the vintage space paraphernalia. And really, all they would need is a few software developers, a ham radio set, and maybe a retired rocket scientist.

Micro-Launch Company

As technology continues to make things smaller
and smaller satellites can now be created with vast
capabilities that are about the size of your fist or
smaller. Today these micro-sats are normally
launched in conjunction with some larger payload.
They just help to fill up a large rocket.

The trouble is that all launch systems of today
are prohibitively expensive even if you are just
piggy-backing. (The launch of a CubeSat can be over
$100,000) The reason the launch systems of today are
so expensive is because most rockets are enormously
complex and expensive machines which only fly once
and are then destroyed. They also require armies of
support to get them prepared and launched and have
to meet very special requirements for the satellite
that they are launching. It is a very high risk
business and an incredibly bloated one.

Large rockets used to be the only way to get
anything into orbit. But since we now have micro-
sats it's time for a micro-launcher.

An opportunity exists to completely re-work the
space launch mantra. Instead of big and expensive,
launches could be made small and cheap with payloads
of just 1-5 pounds using a small disposable
launcher.

After all, since the payloads are cheaper and
require less precision, a company can create a
rocket that they, basically, just point at the sky
and light a fuse. It could be made cheaply and with
far less precision that any of the larger rockets.
More or less it would be an upscaled hobby rocket.

Now, even hobby rockets are not cheap when one
starts to reach for high altitudes. The company that
works with micro-launches will have to be able to
mass produce their vehicle in order to keep the cost
down. Rockets that come off the assembly line in
droves are not a practice anywhere in the space
industry. This is where a scrappy start-up can get
an edge.

Now if a company where to be capable of mass-producing orbital/sub-orbital rockets the single problem they might have is whether the demand will meet the supply. There are not a huge number of satellites being created today. The key in the beginning will be to create alternate reasons to launch. Things like space burials, (cremated remains) time-capsule launches, and other less scientific and broader market reasons to send a rocket to space. These alternate sources of revenue would be able to sustain a company until people realize that satellite launches are cheap enough that they can be performed by smaller hobby groups or even individuals. If the price to launch a CubeSat were brought down to under $10,000 then a whole DIY satellite industry would open up.

Up Aerospace is already working towards this goal of an affordable micro-launcher. They are starting like most new space companies by creating a sounding rocket that is able to launch small experiments into sub-orbital space.

While the mass production of small launchers is a relatively unexplored option the main risk to this business would not be technical problems or even demand. It would be competition from reusable craft like Skylon, a British spaceplane under development, or even a SpaceX upgrade that makes the micro-launcher too expensive. Reusable spacecraft are expected to bring the cost of orbital launches down to around $10-100 per pound within the next twenty years. It is doubtful that even a rocket with the benefit of economy of scale would be able to match that. It is like the difference between buying a Cessna or a 787 for one trip. If you have to buy the whole 787 for the trip then you will buy the Cessna. But if the 787 is just selling a ticket on one trip, then you will ignore the Cessna.

But though a mass produced disposable rocket may become too expensive, the lessons learned from that early part of the business would help to make a small mass produced reusable rocket. One would have to do some deeper number crunching to see what the business margins would be like on this, but it is very likely possible. Not to mention that fact that some micro-sats will pay extra to not have to piggy-back on another satellite.

Overall, the concept of launching ultra-small payloads affordably is untouched. And though the door of opportunity might be closing it has the potential to give someone a chance to get their foot in the door of the industry at a cost significantly less that a full scale launch company.

Space Sports Cars

Ever since the very rich have existed there have been niche markets around their desires. Some of these desires include mansions, yachts, jets, sports cars and even submarines. Why not continue that market philosophy into space by creating luxury or super high quality reusable spacecraft. A space sports car.

Such craft would be very similar to ships like the Lynx or even the SpaceShips One and Two. Small, reusable, and containing proven technology. But the similarity would end there.

Any kind of spaceship that would want to tout itself as a space sports car would have to have many more high-end attributes than the private spaceships currently available.

First, it would have to be able to be crewed by someone who does not have a history of test piloting. After all, the owner would probably want to fly his ship once in awhile.

Next, the ship would likely need to have increased capacity for systems that increase the performance and experience of the flight. These would allow for more "flying" instead of just floating around. Or, maybe, a better "kick" when they launch. No doubt, once having learned to fly the thing, the owners might like to be able to really drive it for a while if in orbit, without worrying about fuel. Feeling the g's and maybe even buzz some space stations.

Lastly, aesthetic design will have to combined with engineering. Much like the Lamborghinis or Ferraris of today. They are not only built for superior function but also superior appearance. While in aerospace, science does lend to beauty slightly, a private spaceplane intended to function as a status symbol or a high performance toy could not look like a Mercury space capsule, though such designs may be optimal. It would have to be sleek and stylish. Custom paint, larger windows, better interiors. Everything about the craft would have to portray beauty and design, not just functionality, in order to increase the value of the experience. This means a departure from only engineers designing craft to bringing in industrial designers and artists to smooth out the rough edges.

Reusability cannot be stressed enough. No one will purchase a 100 million dollar craft that they can only use once or have to spend 10 million on every time it launches no matter how rich they are. Whether orbital or suborbital the craft will have to be as simple to maintain and launch as a private airplane. Multistage will likely be out of the question. Therefore, such craft will likely begin as suborbital planes until technology develops enough for a Single Stage to Orbit (SSTO) system.

This type of company could be started immediately. With the advent of commercial, suborbital spaceplanes only a few years away, it would be possible for a talented engineer and designer to purchase a few of these planes and upgrade them for wealthy, private individuals. This direction will probably be undertaken by companies like Virgin Galactic or even XCOR Aerospace once full production is underway.

Such a company would be able to operate on little initial capital from the founders. The space cars could follow a pre-order system with initial money down, from the customer to start building, and then the rest of it when the project is complete.

As time goes on and the company grows and technology advances, it would be possible for the company to create original or custom designs for its clients. Instead of repurposing spaceplanes they would be able to create original "Lamborghinis of the Void."

Obviously this type of a business is for a niche of a niche. Millionaire or billionaire thrill-seekers. There are only a few of those. Even with his own spaceplane company, Richard Branson would likely invest in a space Lamborghini, but Bill Gates probably wouldn't.

The primary danger with any part of this concept is the market. First, if it is too small. And second, if it has too much liability attached. After all, your craft is meant to reliably transport the wealthiest of the wealthy.

The problem of the small market can be dealt with. Governments and large companies will want ships redesigned for any number of reasons. The beginning custom spaceplane shop would be able to get all kinds of business outside of its wealthy thrill-seeker target market.

As far as the second problem. There is nothing that can be done except to do the best you can and have a good insurance policy and lawyer for when someone crashes their space Ferrari.

Overall, the idea of creating the height of style and performance for space is something that can be accomplished within the next decade without gigantic research or investment. Such an approach would be a good means for talented young engineers and entrepreneurs to make their mark in the space industry in a significant way.

Space Sports

Until such a time as the space industry is able to produce materials and services that allow it to support itself internally, it will have to create products that provide something meaningful to the people on Earth. At this point, the space industry's transfer of material goods to and from space is not exactly a mass market. Even though they help to serve a mass market, (i.e. communication satellites) such activities do not immediately identify a space company as the provider of the service. If the space industry wishes to broaden its horizons it will have to create products and services that can be marketed to the more general population.

So what is a space product or experience that is out of reach to the normal person but can still be enjoyed and paid for by that individual? Well, an Earth equivalent to this situation would be professional football or basketball. Many people aspire to be great athletes but if it is out of their reach they are contented with simply being a fan of the experience. The creation of space sports would create an identical experience. Space sports are an opportunity for the space industry to broaden its horizons beyond launch vehicles and government contracts.

A space sport would have to utilize zero gravity to its greatest potential. This means the players would have to be able to fly and maneuver within a large area. Think of the battle room from the movie "Ender's Game." Normally, large spaces are difficult and expensive to attain in space. Even Bigelow Aerospace's inflatable modules would not do the trick. But it is not necessary to create an interior field for such a sport. With durable space suits and proper safety measures in place the "stadium" could just be a large cage in orbit that keeps the untethered players from flying into oblivion. Such a structure would simple be to design, maintain, and deploy and would be magnitudes cheaper to build than a modern football stadium even with launch costs.

The sport itself would probably be a type of 3-D soccer, where the players pass a ball and attempt to put it through the other team's goal area. But there are no requirements for the sport, it could be dodgeball, or something where the teams have to catch robotic balls. This is a decision that would have to be made by the organization founding the sport.

Human players will be necessary. Since human spectators would not have the same connection to a competition of robots. This means that the facility will have to have attached living spaces for several dozen people. With launches priced at 60 million dollars, the teams will likely have to remain in orbit for the entire "season." Meaning a space station will need to be created at the "stadium" with life support and supplies on a scale that has never been attempted.

The cost of food and the construction of living space will be where the highest costs will come from. But these can be one-time costs if the station is outfitted with amenities like gardens and efficient recycling technologies that will minimize the need for re-supply. This way the station can be built and then becomes almost self-sustaining.

Sports are a great business because, once established, there are so many revenue sources. There are ticket sales, television contracts, advertising, and contracts with vendors. Nearly all of these money streams exist in space as well as on Earth. Television broadcasts of the "Space Matches" will be the primary source of income. As the tourist industry begins to blossom ticket sales will be an option. And, as far as vendors are concerned, for tourists to attend the matches, they will need to be fed and transported just as in stadiums on Earth. Partnerships with such space taxis and suppliers will be inevitable.

The risk involved with space sports is that they are not something that can be proven as "the next big thing." They would be an all or nothing gamble. But space sports have the potential to be a global phenomenon devoid of cultural preference, since it would be the first new sport in nearly a hundred years to define the modern technological age. Its complete novelty would be its advantage. But if no one on the planet appreciates it, it will flop hard.

But the potential of the idea could be tested by simply building the "field" and then sending up a couple of teams to play a few televised games. The investment would be around 200 million dollars, for such a test, but is far less than creating an entire space station. If the response is favorable then the complete "stadium" and living area could be built.

Space sports are something that will eventually come to pass. It is as inevitable as the colonization of Mars. The question is not "if" but "when." It's possible today to prove the concept with a few hundred million dollars. If successful it would give an added boost to the perception of the space industry and space itself and create an entirely new facet in the sports industry. And even though the investment is substantial, when a top professional football team has a value in the area of about 1 billion dollars, revenue of about 350 million dollars, and player expenses around 150 million, the risks and benefits of a Space Sport are nearly identical.

Telepresence Astronaut

Humans are very expensive to maintain in space. Even as launch prices come down the cost of providing food, air, and water to a group of people will always be substantial. Especially in locations such as space stations where there are few natural resource to draw from.

In addition, humans require a great deal of preparation and equipment in order to perform any kind of duty in space. It is not uncommon for astronauts to spend 2-3 hours gearing up for an 8 hour EVA. In commercial applications this time used to just "get ready for work" is unacceptable and un-maintainable. If a group of construction workers is sent to orbit the company that sponsored them does not want them to spend a third of their workday getting ready to start work.

51

The simple solution to all of these problems is to replace the humans. Robots can literally live in space without any of the extra amenities that humans need. But robots are continuously limited by their intelligence. While AI is developing it is still far from rivaling the problem-solving that a human can bring to the table. But robots are able to mimic our physical abilities quite well. Therefore the logical solution would be to create robots which are remotely operated by humans. Therefore one ends up with, basically, a robot with the mind of a human, which needs no food, water, or preparation to start work,

Virtual reality has progressed far enough that it is possible for a human to have a completely immersive experience while operating a robot. The controller can see through the eyes of the machine and watch as the robot arms mimic the controller's motions so perfectly that the person can feel as if they are in a suit in space.

This type of telecontrol eliminates the need for people to go to space at all to perform duties. Thus greatly reducing cost and risk to any company which ventures into this sector. The robots would risk the launch and the environment, the controller would operate from 9 to 5 as if they were in orbit, but then have dinner at home.

Fortuitously, this technology has been an area of study for NASA for some time. Robonaut is essentially all that has just been discussed and is currently operating on the ISS in a limited capacity. Much of this research is in the public domain and could be utilized by a start-up wishing to develop a telepresence astronaut to fill the stated needs.

Of course, anyone wishing to pursue such an endeavor would not need to begin with a full humanoid and virtual reality set-up. The company could start with small space drones which could be remotely operated and used to inspect spacecraft and perhaps even act as a defense against large space debris. This is a relatively simple and inexpensive system to produce and deploy.

As the need for human workers or equivalents grows, with the advent of space stations and interplanetary craft, more advanced robots can be created. These could begin service as emergency responders and maintenance workers where time for human preparation is not available. This time advantage will be something any company would be able to flaunt around. If a space station develops a fault which must quickly be repaired from the outside which would one rather have? A human who needs two hours to get to the problem or a robot which needs two minutes.

Concerning business structure, such robots would likely be deployed on a rental basis. A space station being constructed could use one for assembly and inspection and when finished the robots would migrate to the next job. Since it needs no food or life support the machine could literally float in orbit for years waiting for the next job. When the emergency benefits of such robots are realized many will be purchased and installed permanently in structures just as one would install a fire extinguisher.

The beauty of such a business is that it is a solution which can be created and then just sit and wait for the demand. A company could send several robots into orbit and have them available when the first private structures are contracted. In the meantime they could be contracted to maintain some satellites and perform checks on existing space vehicles.

Essentially, such a robotics firm would likely begin as an orbital safety drone provider. It would have the job of checking ships before they re-enter the atmosphere and ensuring there are no fatal flaws. Then as the construction industry grows they can develop into telepresence bodies for astronauts who are Earth-bound or restricted to their space vehicle. After that who knows? Machines with men inside could be created that prepare colony sites for human occupation.

A market exists now for such space safety drones. If they had existed earlier the Columbia accident could have been avoided. And since a robot is cheaper to send to space than a human the market for a telepresence astronaut will come and grow.

It is a sector with a proven need and proven technology. All the ground work has been laid by other entities; it simply needs to be turned into a business. And until launch costs come far down and human equipment develops much further this will be an integral service in the space industry.

Orbital Zoning

For nearly sixty years humans have been sending objects into orbit. Some are weather satellites, others digital TV, and some are just junk. Though there is a huge volume of orbital space above Earth to put satellites in, orbits are in fact filling up and and are largely uncontrolled. As the private space industry grows the need to zone and regulate orbits for particular uses and organizations will be increasingly necessary to create a safe and effective orbital airspace.

To clarify this concept let's look at a scenario. Imagine a company, such as Bigelow Aerospace, has constructed an orbital hotel. The station sits in an orbit several hundred miles above Earth. Now another company developing a space BattleBots show decided to set up shop in the same orbit. This is allowed because no one owns the orbit or can prohibit anyone else form using it. Unfortunately, the Spacebots end up smashing each other to pieces in the orbit, much to the enjoyment of Earth spectators. But now there is an increase of debris which could easily puncture the soft hull of the space station. While the Spacebots would be held accountable for the damage the entire problem could have been avoided if the space station was able to zone its orbit for only human occupation. This is a slightly silly circumstance but the point is clear.

The same type of situation is the reason that factories can't be built in residential areas here on Earth. Similar rules must be set up for space. It will not be possible for space to continually be treated as an international free area like Antarctica. Unlike Antarctica, people and organizations actually want to go to space and get something from it, in this case a location.

Orbits are real estate, just as on Earth. There are certain locations better suited for certain tasks and some that are filled with dangerous litter. But there are a lot of orbits above the Earth. The 3-D nature of space allows for this, as well as the fact that everything in orbit is moving and can be coordinated.

So how does one go about defining property in a place where there are no boundaries just the "idea" of locations?

Well the simple place to begin would be with altitude. Space could be divided into more altitude layers. Within those altitudes one could then define particular orbits just as radio bands are defined on Earth. Particular altitudes could be reserved for Earth observation, others for communications satellites, and then the areas above the debris-filled orbits could be reserved for space stations.

Then within the altitudes particular orbital trajectories could be defined. A company would be able to purchase these trajectories and maintain its hardware within them. But this opens the question, from whom does one purchase an orbit, something which transcends any type of Earth boundary.

The likely solution would be to allow for homesteading of defined orbits. Organizations and countries could agree to allow ownership of particular orbits through a system of placing improvements in them. Then once ownership of an orbit has been established, through the International Homesteading System, the orbits can be sold. This does require international cooperation but that is the case in many aspects of Space Law and a topic for another time.

Enforcement of homesteading boundaries will be an issue. How to keep vehicles in their space and ensure no one trespasses will initially fall to ground-based tracking and monitoring of payloads as they are launched. But eventually a Space Authority will have to be established to act as a "traffic cop" for Earth orbits. It would go around checking the authorizations of certain satellites to be in certain areas and perhaps "towing" them when they are not.

The issue of spy satellites will also be a problem. These craft are some of the best kept secrets in the world. Governments will not want to register spy satellites or even relegate them to particular altitudes. But as slowly as orbital space is filling this issue may resolve itself before it has to be addressed for private needs.

Space will eventually have to have a system of organization or regulation. Responsibility for space debris and sharing of orbits will become too large of issues to simply ignore. Orbits will become crowded and at that point everyone will want to know what is theirs, else the industry could become quite confrontational. This can't happen because it would be self-defeating to the development of a pace economy.

Note: A particular example of where zoning of orbits would have been useful would have been in the Chinese Satellite Missile Test incident. Again, it is an issue of international relations but if the Space-Faring nations had collaborated to allocate weapons testing orbits, other nations and organizations could have avoided those areas and now not have to dodge debris.

Space Arena

Space stations are one of the most expensive propositions in the private space industry. The only one in operation today is the ISS and it is estimated to have cost $150 billion in construction and occupation expenses. Certainly, the construction of the ISS is a poor example, especially when comparing to some technologies in the private sector. SpaceX is reducing cost of launching stations and Bigelow Aerospace is making stations simpler to build and deploy. But even so, constructing a "building" in orbit is not a cheap or easy proposition no matter how you look at it today.

The cost of a space stations is not all that surprising. After all it is something which has to provide all of the comforts of home (i.e. food, air, water) with none of the resources. It has to keep humans alive in one of the most inhospitable places for life that we know.

But does a space station really need to provide all of these resources in order to have value? What is a space station really for in the private space industry, as far as money-generating options?

A space station can be a place to rent space to companies to perform experiments in zero-g. It can become a space hotel to paying tourists. It can be a stop-over to someplace else.

These are all very viable industries once people gain a greater presence in space. But again, all of these "products" for a station to act as are incredibly expensive. Because they are meant to separate a person from the outside.

But if someone is going to go to space for the experience, they probably will not want to be separated from the outside by a cramped station or capsule. They will want to get the full benefit of the absence of gravity and the views of the planet and stars.

So why not build a station that doesn't protect anyone from the elements but instead just keeps them from getting lost. Build a station that is basically a giant cage.

Such a structure would basically be a Space Arena. A huge playing field where spacefarers can get the EVA experience without the safety hazards.

From a design standpoint it could be a huge geodetic structure which deploys to create a faceted sphere which is covered in a soft mesh that keeps things and people from floating away. Easy to build, deploy, and maintain. All of which decrease the cost of the station.

Instead of having to launch it in sections it could be launched in a single unit, perhaps on a Falcon Heavy, and then literally just sit there. Since it wouldn't require any complex life support systems those would not have to be maintained and, since space has no other stresses than changes in temperature, there is nothing to wear out the station structurally. And other resources such as the development of orbital tugboats become available, it wouldn't even be necessary to have much of an attitude control system.

With this kind of station all the travelers need is a spacesuit to keep them protected from the elements and a capsule to go sleep in. Both of which are already necessary for the trip. So why have a station which is a repeat of both of the other two just on another scale.

Since the permeable station is easier to construct and maintain is easier to make large. The size of such permeable stations allows them to be used by industries that have yet to consider space. The station could be used as a playing field for a space sport, creating a viable return and interest to people on Earth. It also gives a complete "space experience" to any tourists, much more effectively that a standard station. Just imagine the difference between seeing the curvature of the Earth through a porthole and being able to have a panoramic view as you fly, un-tethered in the ether.

The experience and the low cost that such a "Space Arena" provides makes it a viable entry into the industry by many companies other than the standard aerospace and research firms. It is something that could be pursued by the entertainment or sports industry.

The business model for the company which owns the station could take any number of forms. If the station was built for space tourism it could be like a low cost motel. Travelers pay to use the space during the trip. If it is created to host space sporting events then it may pay for itself through the interest and entertainment value of the sport.

If you consider the "Space Arena" to be something akin to a stadium in orbit for sporting events it is actually much cheaper than Earth-bound stadiums which run anywhere from $500 million into the billions. Whereas the cost to build and launch the Space arena would likely be only $150-200 million dollars. Still a huge gamble but it also has more utility and range of markets than a basketball stadium does.

The creation of a "Space Area" is something which really has very few technical hurdles. It is really a matter of "just doing it." The only things for a company or entrepreneur to consider with such a station is that it can increase the risk of a standard space excursion. Imagine someone in a space suit pushing off of one side of the sphere and then colliding hard with a structural member on the other side and perhaps over-straining their spacesuit causing it to rupture. Safety will be a huge concern for such a venture but materials and designs do exist which can help to mitigate most of these risks.

As far as space stations go the concept of a "Space Arena" or permeable space station are concepts which are relatively unexplored and potentially underestimated. They are a structure which can be easily and cheaply constructed and can be used to create a fantastic space experience both for those utilizing the station and to those on Earth, if it is used for televised sporting events.

Space to Earth Delivery

Currently most of the effort in the space industry is toward getting things into space. However, there will come a time when we will be trying to bring more stuff down from space. Materials mined from asteroids, completed manufactured goods, finished experiments, and other products that were mined, grown, or made in space will require a means to bring them back down.

NASA has already begun addressing this problem. Intuitive Machines' Terrestrial Return Vehicle is being completed and is intended to begin testing on the ISS in 2016. The purpose of the vehicle will be to provide a quick means to deliver time sensitive experiments safely back to Earth where further analysis can take place which can't occur on the space station. The design is expected to be launched from the station and then maneuver to and land at the nearest spaceport.

Delivery from space is a very viable business opportunity. Especially since commercial space stations, primarily from Bigelow Aerospace, are only a maximum of 5-10 years away. While NASA is taking the approach of creating a special vehicle for the task that is not the only method or business model.

A delivery company from space could begin as simply an organizer. Buying space on returning capsules for materials from other space stations. This would actually change the business dynamic of commercial launches, who's operation generally relies on only one ticket, round-trip or one way, to one customer. As traffic increases one organization can purchase the trip up but then someone else can reserve the trip down.

The reason NASA and Intuitive Machines are creating a single miniature craft for the task of delivery from orbit is schedule flexibility. Renting space on a capsule is fettered with the schedule of the capsule launch. But cargo, particularly experiments, may have expiration dates. The TRV ensures rapid delivery whenever needed. Just like Amazon, same-day delivery is the Holy Grail.

So what is required for a technology that drops things from orbit on command and lands them safely? This is dependent on the cargo. The TRV is a small craft for delivering small experiments. The small size allows for multiple craft to be delivered to the ISS in a single launch. The TRV is also outfitted with a maneuvering system. It is basically a complete small spaceship.

The complete spaceship design for the TRV is acceptable for the current state of the art and the amount of cargo transported. But as time passes completely disposable spaceships may be too expensive. An alternate method could be something along the lines of a space gun which launches small capsules of goods which are delivered from locations in orbit. This would eliminate the need for internal propulsion of the capsules and may simplify capsule design from lifting body to the more common tear-drop shape. Though such a system would not be required for several decades. Until inter-orbit transportation and exchange is common. Basically the "space gun" would be the post office and there would be mailmen going around orbit picking up "packages" and delivering them to the "space gun."

Going even a step further and considering asteroid mining. At some point the materials within those rocks will have to be delivered to Earth if they are to have any value. The trouble is that most asteroids burn up as they enter our atmosphere. A method will have to be devised for delivering these rocks safely to the surface so their contents can be collected and sold. Something along the lines of an ablative blanket could be created which protects the asteroids from the heat of reentry. (Similar to how asteroid miners plan to protect water rocks from the sun's heat) Or perhaps large skeletal landers could be created which have a heat shield and a parachute. These landers could be filled with mined material or raw asteroids and landed, then, perhaps, even reused.

While all the focus has been on getting into space the need to send stuff back is growing every day. The ISS needs to return experiments. Planetary Resources may need to land rocks. Private space stations may need to return manufactured goods. There may even be a need to send parts down to Earth to be repaired and returned at the next launch of a capsule.

In order to develop an economy in space a two-way exchange between Earth and space must be set-up. Getting up there is great, but it matters little to the world unless something comes back.

Orbital Data Centers

Cloud computing is the idea of storing data on a server or having that server perform tasks so there is less load on your computer. But these servers are located in warehouses on Earth. They require large amounts of energy, they have a large footprint, and they have to transmit data over a distance to your computer. What if server farms were placed into orbit? What if cloud computing occurred above the clouds?

Orbital server farms would have several benefits to their terrestrial counterparts. The first is power. In orbit there is an abundant supply of solar energy, twice as much as what enters our atmosphere and hits the ground. It is also possible to be in continuous sunlight. This provides a clean and inexhaustible power supply for the farm.

Next, there is an abundant amount of space in space. A server farm may grow as large as or larger than any building on Earth.

Last, concerning transmission time, space really is halfway to anywhere. Today and in the future satellite transmission will be common. The trip up and then back down takes only millionths of a second but that is very slow for a computer which works with billions of operations per second. Halving the distance of transmission by just sending information

down, instead of up then down, would increase
internet speeds.

But that is a far rosier picture than reality.
While endless solar power is available in orbit it
would still require huge arrays to power a server
farm. The ISS solar array is the size of a football
field and provides 110 kilowatts of energy, enough
to power 55 houses. But a 55,000 square foot server
farm on Earth uses 5 megawatts or enough to power
5000 homes. Clearly a development in space power
systems will need to be built. But computing is
becoming more efficient all the time so such power
requirements may not remain standard.

Next, indeed a server farm may grow as large as
it wishes in orbit. But with increased size comes
increased weight and therefore higher launch costs.
The cost of space launches would have to become a
thousand times cheaper than the cheapest SpaceX
launcher existing today in order to compete with
terrestrial installment. However initial launch
costs may be offset if lifetime power costs were
lower due to orbital solar plants.

Last, while internet and communication speeds may
be twice as fast by placing the servers in orbit
this may not be a significant enough trade-off for
the risks of creating such a facility. But Google
and others are working on using satellites to
provide internet connectivity to the world, adding a
few servers to the satellites is not a great leap.

But perhaps the biggest problem of all to such
facilities may be cooling. Servers become very hot
and require constant removal of heat. But in space
there are few options for heat removal. Heat can
only leave by radiation. But a satellite using solar
power is also constantly absorbing heat as thermal
radiation. If a satellite also has a hot server farm
at its center then a substantial thermal management
problem arises.

Despite those challenges here is why such data
centers will exist. Just as Google and Facebook are
trying to provide internet connectivity to places
where there is none, so to do they need to provide

data storage and computation. Second, having large power hogging facilities in orbit will reduce the load on Earth power plants and not be in danger of blackouts while using the Sun's energy. Last, if humans go to Mars they will need computing power. But it makes no sense to attempt to land servers on Mars when they can perform just as well in orbit and perhaps provide services to multiple settlements. The same goes for the Moon. The effort of landing a server farm on another body is too great when it can just be parked in orbit.

The latter scenarios may be where orbital computing systems begin. Providing computing resources to future Mars missions. Small server farms requiring nothing on the scale of terrestrial data centers could be created and then launched to support space missions. This is something that already has many engineering precedents in places like the ISS. It a project which is well within current technologies to achieve and could actually be built by a small firm or just a few people in a garage. From there such orbital data centers could follow a modular growth plan where new, self-contained modules are continuously combined to create ever large server farms which are able to finally provide meaningful quantities of computation to the world or other colonies.

Data centers in space are something which have potential and are currently feasible. However in order to scale them to compete with existing data centers in a substantial way requires growth and construction of other space resources. However, small scale orbital server farms can be created to support missions to other planets which will be coming in the next decades. Whether they will ever replace their cousins on the ground on Earth is unknowable until the industry develops more.

Moon

Lunar Retirement Home

As people grow old they begin to become a bit decrepit. Normal everyday tasks can present dangers of heart attacks, strokes or a broken bone from a fall. The pull of gravity puts so much strain on the elderly that many lose almost all of their independence for fear of being killed by the pull of the Earth.

Fortunately, though we may not control gravity there are places, which will come within reach, where gravity is not such a predominant force. The closest is the Moon.

So here is the opportunity. Within the next 50-100 years space entrepreneurs have the chance to create a retirement colony on the Moon.

On the lunar surface the gravity is 1/6 that of Earth. There would no longer be the danger of falls or strains on the hearts of the residents. They would be able to live independently, almost as they had before they aged, being able to do their own chores, walk, and even run.

Now the question is why is the Moon ideal for such a structure? Why not just put people into orbit in a large space station where there is zero gravity.

First, the change of going from gravity to zero gravity, permanently, can be a large strain on such elderly bodies. The deterioration could be too extreme as the body adapts to the environment. There is also a learning curve for operating in zero-g. Floating and navigating in a weightless environment takes skills, reflexes, and coordination that the elderly may no longer have. The gravity of the moon doesn't require people to change their habits. They can still walk and run, it will simply be easier. The Moon is also within communications range of the Earth so the tenants can still remain in practically real-time contact with their families and friends.

The Moon will also offer the advantage of unlimited ways to spend time. Hikes, tours, sports and other activities that cannot be performed by the resident on Earth or by a space station in orbit are available on the Moon. What better place to retire than where there is always something to do and is continuously beautiful.

The last reason to use the Moon is that the retirement center can be made more cheaply and safely on the Moon than in orbit. This is due to the fact that the Moon will have a construction infrastructure that will be able to build and expand facilities using the materials on the Moon. So instead of having to launch everything, for the center, from Earth, as in the case of the space station, it can be manufactured on site. This infrastructure also makes the facility safer than any orbital facility could be. If a leak is sprung, the residents could be moved out into new spaces, which are constructed, or share with other colonists, in an emergency. A space station does not have this luxury of places to go.

Now for the dangers of such an endeavor. Space medicine is still unclear as to the complete effects of low gravity on the human body, and it is completely unknown what it will do to an elderly body. While the physical abilities will be improved, internally we don't know what can happen. Low gravity can cause the bones to give off huge amounts of calcium into the body which form kidney stones and other ailments. Who knows what this type of thing would do to the elderly body.

There is also the question of transport. Launch and journey to the Moon can be relatively violent procedures that can put great stresses on the body. The only hope will be that conveyances like space elevators can become feasible in order to create a gentle journey.

Overall, the idea of a retirement community on the moon is one of the riskier endeavors to attempt with the technology we understand today. But it is feasible and potentially very lucrative with the advent of cheaper launches and bases on the Moon. While it is still decades away current doctors and engineers can work to create the medical needs for such a concept today.

The Moon is the Best Start

Since having gone to the Moon, the public and the space community have begun to ignore it. Instead they have set their sights on the new frontier of Mars. And though the colonization of Mars is an important target, both from the perspective of human exploration and preservation, it is not a place where a return can be easily had from a business perspective. The facts that it is the most similar planet to Earth in the solar system, and some distance away, are its downfalls. A space economy will not need another Earth; we have plenty to go around as it is. The future space economy will need a place that can serve as an independent base, which has unique characteristics that make it more viable than the red rock of Mars or the cold metal of a space station. Such a place will be the Moon. The Moon holds far more advantages to the creation of the first economically thriving colony than any other potential location in the solar system. The Moon should be the colonization target of the private space industry.

The number one reason the Moon is the most ideal place to create a permanent settlement in space is its proximity to Earth. The Moon is only a few days away with 1960's spaceships. This allows the Moon to have a very flexible trade route and exchange with Earth. If there is a problem help can arrive in days. If a piece of equipment is needed, it's only a phone call away. Mars, on the other hand, will take months to travel to, and currently requires relatively precise timing in order to make the trip as efficient as possible. If you miss a particular launch window one would have to wait several months or years before another would arrive. Plus its distance creates a time dilation in transmissions

68

that makes that part of the process slow and inconvenient.

But the proximity to Earth doesn't just aide travel time. It also decreases the risk to the people that work on the Moon. Though the Moon has no atmosphere and is barren rock exposed to space, it is still semi-protected by the Earth's magnetic field. This field decreases the overall radiation that hits the Moon's surface, as well as the ships traveling to and from it. This protective force field disappears as a ship travels to Mars. Though radiation is still present in heightened quantities on the Moon, one will sustain far less exposure than during a six month trip to Mars.

The Moon's desolation is also a very valuable resource. There is no drag from air to slow launches and a sixth the force of gravity. These characteristics make it relatively simple and efficient to move material to and from the Moon's surface. This allows trade with passing ships and easy transport of cargo. These conditions also allow for launch technologies other than rockets. Rail guns and space elevators are viable systems on the Moon. All of this can create a functioning spaceport. A place where ships can land, launch, resupply, and even be built. Such possibilities as these are not viable on Mars because its similarity to Earth creates the same complications for spacecraft we have on Earth. And again it is too far away to quickly and efficiently build what would be needed at first.

One the most valuable parts of the Moon is its physical resources. The regolith of the Moon can be turned into any number of construction materials. Concrete blocks, sintered beams, rail tracks, these are all items that can be made from the lunar dust. The Moon also has deposits of water. This allows the colony to support its inhabitants without constant resupply. Water allows for farming, showers, and the creation of rocket fuel. (a very useful thing in space) Any base built on the Moon, with sufficient power emplacements, can continually grow and

manufacture from the resources available. And the
base is able to get from the Earth whatever it can't
make, since the Moon is close enough to have an
Amazon account. The resources and the proximity of
the Moon allow a lunar colony to not only sustain
itself but also create a surplus that can be traded
to other space-farers. Options such as space
stations have no ability to grow past what is
provided.

The Moon also has a special advantage over Mars
or a space station as a tourist attraction. It's low
gravity and epic landscapes create an experience
that is unmatched. Any colony may be able to ease
the financial burden by allowing "guests" to spend
time there during a two week vacation. Again
proximity to Earth lends a hand.

Any early lunar colony would also be a target for
funding from any number of scientific fields.
Astronomy, physics, biology. A colony with excess
facilities would be able to lease out space to to
astronomers looking for an unobstructed view of the
stars and others like them. And since the Moon lends
its materials to creating excess space, this option
would be a low cost, high return proposition for an
established colony. Mars doesn't have the view and
space stations don't have the space.

Lastly, the Moon has something that can be
utilized on Earth, this is a necessary
characteristic for any early space economy. Just
like the missions to the Americas by the Hudson Bay
Company, they didn't pay for themselves with
exploration, but with exploitation, the same idea
must be adopted here. The Moon has minerals such as
Helium-3. This isotope is an ideal fuel for fusion,
once the process is perfected, but is practically
non-existent on Earth. The Moon is full of the
stuff, due to the solar radiation that hits its
surface. This material and others like it would be
the tradable good that can be brought back from the
Moon and sold on the Earth. As far as we know, Mars
has no unique or valuable resources to draw from
with a potential financial return.

Overall, the Moon is just a more reliable place to create something that can actually have an economic presence. Its resources allow for surplus creation and tradable products. Its proximity to Earth allows for easy and quick transportation. Its gravity and lack of atmosphere allow for easy interaction with other facets of the space community. And its environment allows for recreational value as well as reduced health risks. Space Stations, Asteroids, and Mars do not have the combination of qualities required to serve as the first true human settlement focused on economic return. Though all will be needed and are necessary steps in the conquest of space. Anyone working to create the ideal spaceport, to be the center of the space economy, should set-up shop on the Moon.

Space Gas Station

In order to create spacecraft, that can move around in Earth orbit and even to other planets, they have to have their tanks filled. Currently, any spacecraft in orbit goes until it runs out of fuel, then it plummets to the Earth. Any manned spacecraft, like the ISS, must be refueled on a regular basis and is limited to Earth orbit since that is where the gauge hits empty for all current space vehicles. The creation of a "Space Gas Station" would create the ability to increase the operational longevity of current spacecraft as well as create a means for current capsules to top themselves off and move on into new missions.

If one is to look at some mission beyond Earth orbit, (Apollo or a Mars mission) normally, the procedure is to carry all the fuel required for the entire mission on a single launch vehicle. This is the equivalent to loading your car with all the fuel needed for a cross country trip. Such strategies greatly increase the cost of launch, especially when present prices are in the neighborhood of $10,000/lb. Certainly launches will become more economical in coming years as prices decrease, but there is still no reason to fill a vehicle with fuel when it could be filled with equipment or other supplies. True, the tanks will still exist, but the "Gas Station" would allow for smaller tanks on vehicles since journeys to fuel sources would be a bit shorter. Again, imagine a car going across country, but now with some gas stations along the way. Now you don't have to carry extra fuel or have such a large tank.

The primary issue with such a service, considering current launch technologies, is that the cost to lift the fuel for the "Gas Station" into orbit is identical to the cost of putting it up with the craft in the first place. For one-mission vehicles this is true. But what about satellites that need to maintain orbits, the ISS, an orbital taxi, or for the space shuttle to be boosted to a higher orbit, if it were still in service. In all of these cases the "Gas Station" makes a lot of sense. If a vehicle needs more fuel to continue a mission or to begin anew, then a location to refill is worth the price. Especially, when the other option is to organize a whole launch to refuel or build and launch an entirely new craft to replace the empty one.

For an example of a situation, where this would be usable today, imagine if a SpaceX Dragon capsule wanted to continue to Mars. Normally the capsule burns all of its fuel to reach orbit, so that is its operational limit. If a "Gas Station" existed, the capsule could dock with it in orbit, fill up, and then fire its engines to break free of Earth gravity. This is, in fact, a maneuver that missions such as Mars One may need to consider, but are only possible with a fuel station in place.

So the need for an orbital "Gas Station" certainly exists, even today. So what would it look like? If the Space Shuttle were still in operation one would assume that it could simply be one of the Shuttles' orange external tanks that was left in orbit and has since been refilled. But that is no longer an option. In the near future the creation of such a fuel depot would most likely require a series of launches with a Falcon Heavy hoisting filled tanks into orbit. These tanks could then either be combined into a single structure or spread throughout orbit to allow easier access to the fuel reserves.

In order to refuel craft, organizations would schedule dockings with the fuel stations through the operating company. Then they would fuel-up and pay based on the amount that they take. It would be identical to a normal Earth gas station.

In the beginning it would be necessary for the craft/organization in need of fuel to navigate to the fuel depot. But as the company operating the station grows it would be possible to implement mobile stations which go to where the fuel is needed or even to implement a team of drones to bring craft to it.

The technical challenges of such a project are significant. Rocket fuel is very hard to contain in large quantities for extended periods of time. Containing large quantities in orbit will be even more difficult. Then there is the problem of actually having the adapters needed to refuel the numerous variations of spacecraft. This will require the eventual creation on some type of standard across the industry.

Such an endeavor will require significant investment in early development and then the first launches. However, once the station is operational, the returns will come quickly, since the price of the fuel will be a markup of the delivery cost to orbit. Such a station would likely only need to be emptied a few times to offset the cost of development and construction. One would have to determine the value, of the fuel, to organizations that want to give second chances to old craft, instead of launching new ones.

The expansion capabilities of such a fuel company would be unlimited. As the industry grows and space traffic increases multiple stations will need to operate in orbit and eventually around other planets. And as mining grows and water ice is brought back to Earth or the Moon the fuel stations can be filled with the refined hydrogen and oxygen. Thus reducing the price of the fuel.

These stations will become the waterholes of space. People will need and want to be near them. Because of this they could be the structures that space hotels and space docks are built off of in order to reduce the number of stops for human vehicles. Rental of such proximity space or connections will become lucrative for the company that owns the gas station.

Though the creation and implementation of an orbital fuel depot will be significant, it is a piece of infrastructure that will be so vital to the space industry that it will quickly pay itself off. It will be as important as the launch vehicles that carry the craft off of the Earth. While some billionaires are building space hotels and others the launch vehicles, it would not be a bad business decision to create a Space Gas Station.

Space Water Refinery

In space, water is liquid gold. It is the heart of all life and of many space technologies by serving as a source of rocket fuel. But how does one get water in space? Water is actually quite plentiful in our solar system. It exists as ice on Mars and the Moon, inside of some asteroids, and is actually a primary component in comets. But, for any of this ice to be made usable by spaceships and colonies, it has to be extracted, melted, and even broken apart at an atomic level. While extraction is being developed by mining companies, the actual refinement of water into either drinkable liquid or rocket fuel has yet to be commercially developed, but such a "Water Refinery" would be an incredibly integral part of a developing space economy.

Water is the very basis of life. Humans can only survive a matter of days without it. This makes it one of the primary consumables on any manned space mission. The trouble is, at this point the only source of water for spacefarers is the Earth. Any water any astronaut drinks has to be shipped to them on an incredibly expensive rocket. Certainly, once the water is in space it can be recycled many times and reused by travelers, but the fact that water had to be blasted into space in the first place is a practice that can't continue. As more people begin to operate in space the need for drinkable water will increase and it will no longer be viable to get it all from Earth.

That is just drinking water. There is also a market for the creation of rocket fuel. Currently, numerous satellites fall to Earth because they run out of gas. And, as planetary travel grows there will be the need to fuel a fleet of rocket ships. As before, fuel can be created on Earth and then launched into space to fuel all these craft. And with dropping launch costs that will be an option. But, the components of water, hydrogen and oxygen, are actually the most efficient rocket fuel that exists.

The technology to split water into these elements (electrolysis) has existed for many years and similar processes have been researched for applications in Mars colonies by NASA. So, instead of shipping fuel from Earth it would actually be possible to just grab a passing comet and turn its water into rocket fuel at a fraction of the cost of launching it.

Of course, there are many operations that have to be in place before a refinery can begin work. The bodies with water have to be mapped. They have to be collected, that is, brought to the refinery. Then, once under control, the asteroid/comet actually has to have the ice mined from its rock and metal.

Fortunately, these are all operations that are being developed and perfected by existing space mining companies. Planetary Resources and Deep Space

Industries are space start-ups that have begun to develop the technologies needed to mine asteroids and comets and even process the materials. They both expect to have operating hardware in space within the next decade. This will give the creators of a space refinery plenty of time to develop their own final product. And they will be able to focus on taking water ice and turning it into liquid water and rocket fuel.

The main resource required by such a facility will be power. It must have copious amounts of electricity available to melt the mined ice, run it through filters for drinking, and perform electrolysis on it to create rocket fuel. This means that the main part of such an operation will be its power plant.

Early on it will most likely run on large solar arrays either connected to the facility itself or provided by a space utility company. It may be possible, and certainly preferable, to use nuclear energy if such technology is allowed into space as the industry develops.

While such a refinery will need storage for its product, that may be a flexible option depending upon other developments in the industry. It may be possible for the refinery to partner with space gas stations or tankers which will be able to handle the storage and delivery issues associated with such a venture. Though if the pockets of the company are deep enough it could become the equivalent of an oil company here on Earth which handles every part of the production process. From extraction of the raw material to putting it in a customer's tank.

So the overall operation of such a refinery would be something along these lines. Someone goes out and collects the raw water ice from asteroids and brings it to the refinery. The refinery, which operates in planetary orbit, either purchases the ice or enters some kind of shared profit system with the mining company. The refinery is equipped with the power and storage facilities it needs to process the ice into drinkable water and fuel. This is then sold to companies that wish to keep satellites in orbit longer or to power ships onto new worlds. The model is identical to an oil company and will require great cooperation between space companies since the creation of all levels of production simultaneously by a single entity would be far too expensive.

Though getting such a company started may not be as difficult as it seems. If one were looking to start small and grow to become "The Space Refinery" it would be prudent to begin by creating and manufacturing small life-support systems that can be used by single craft or small bases to make drinkable water and purify existing supplies. This would create demand for the company in the current space industry.

Then, as permanent bases and long range re-usable craft begin to be developed, the refinery company could develop the fuel creation system. The two variations of the technology could be used in places such as early moon bases like a backyard still. Such a strategy would make the company a major contributor to the industry early on and give it the position it needs to implement a larger-scale independent refinery in space when the demand arises.

Drinkable water and rocket fuel are the two primary consumables for anyone that operates in space. Any spacecraft must have fuel and any human must have water. The water needed to meet both of these needs is present in the void of space and can be exploited. The only thing that is required is an individual(s) that will work to become the "Water Baron" of space by creating the water refineries needed to exploit this abundant and necessary resource.

Space Garden

Long term space occupation is currently limited by the supply chain. The ISS has to be refueled and restocked multiple times a year to keep just a few people alive and fed for small periods of time. While the cost of launching supplies is going down, such disposability of resources is not a sustainable means of developing a large space economy and society.

Food is one of the largest consumables on the space station. Food mass is comparable to, or even greater than fuel. Food is the resource that can't be easily recycled or reused, even with modern technology. And even though there were old proposals to use human waste as radiation shielding and other such applications, these have never been implemented and most likely never will be. Space food, in its current state, also adds unnecessary bulk and weight to missions. At this point if a mission were to be launched to Mars an entire capsule would have to be stuffed with protein bars and freeze dried-spaghetti.

But food and the waste it creates can be recycled and reused; it simply requires something a bit less sterile than the systems currently in use. Space missions need to adopt a more organic means of food production and recycling in order to reduce bulk and increase reusability.

Ignoring the technical challenges for a moment, if a space garden could be implemented into a space station or capsule it would have benefits far beyond just food production and recycling. An obvious one would be the purification of air though plants' natural processes. NASA has also performed research that proves that the cultivation of plants while in isolation, i.e. a space capsule, has positive psychological effects on humans. Plants and other living things create a connection with Earth that helps the astronauts feel more at home in space. If appropriately arranged plants would also offer the organic radiation shielding long considered by space technologists.

So that is the market. The creation of an agricultural center for a space station which can produce food and recycle the waste, while providing as many of the side benefits as possible.

Now on to the technical side of the space garden. Weight is always a concern, but one would be able to get around this by developing a system that has a lifetime weight savings if it is able to produce food from seed to plate thereby reducing the cost of transportation.

Creating a garden in space is not quite as simple as just sending up some pots and putting seeds in them. If a space garden is to have maximum impact it has to have a complete cycle built into it. Astronauts plant the food, the food grows, astronauts eat the food, and then what is left is put back into the garden. While this has been a common practice on Earth for millennia, in space where an entire ecosystem is difficult to create, there will have to be technological systems in place that help turn waste into compost. These could be filtering mechanisms or possibly a bio-reactor that can break down human waste to a form that is more sanitary to work with.

The system would have to be clean, one of the banes of space gardens. Too much delicate machinery has to be protected from stray dirt or water. This means that any type of garden would need to be in a self-contained module. The "module" could range in size from that of a habitat to just the size of a trunk.

Those are some basic considerations. But if the developer of such a space garden wants to maximize some of the other benefits they must go beyond a garden-in-a-box. They may want to leave food production out of it and simply create a biological recycling system. This would mean a focus on the ability of the plants to use human waste to create pure air. This could lead to something like a large tank of algae. If one were truly imaginative they might find a way to turn the algae into food. But if the psychological aspect is the focus maybe a special type of flower would be more appropriate. A space garden can have many variations and focuses, and therefore a large potential product base.

A truly universal space garden would likely be an entire self-contained module which is something that is added to a space station and not simply parked on a shelf. This would most likely be where a young start-up would begin. Building entire gardens designed to sustain a crew with food, air, and fulfillment during a mission to Mars. Then as the space industry grows the size of the garden could be reduced in order to accommodate different missions and needs which require more variability and smaller scales.

A space garden also has the advantage of being one of the technologies which does not need to go to space to be perfected. Plants can be chosen, tests run, and systems tested in a terrestrial environment very easily. This makes the cost of development relatively small compared to other space technologies and increases the possibility of pre-orders that can offset start-up costs.

The creation of a space garden can be far less technical than the creation of a rocket engine. But it does take a level of know-how that easily creates a competitive advantage. Sustenance farming in isolation has not been practiced in the capitalistic world for some time. The tricks of the trade may be harder to find than just a few agriculture students. But it can be done and is something that would be immensely valuable to the space industry by reducing transportation cost of food, rising morale in space, and performing cleaning of an environment that rapidly becomes stuffy. This is an opportunity that has hardly been pursued by anyone in the industry, public or private, but it will gain much more attention in the future.

Lunar Space Elevator

A space elevator will likely never be implemented in our lifetime on Earth. Space junk, material sciences, and general liability will all prohibit it from being a feasible system using any of the methods proposed thus far.

However, the space elevator is still incredibly viable in other locations. Small moons and large asteroids which have gravity but no atmosphere or space trash are ideal for space elevators. Since a space elevator can run off of electricity and is not limited by refueling or controlling explosions, it is far more reliable as a method of shipping items to and from orbit around a body.

The body most ideal for the first true space elevator will likely be the Moon. The Moon is a clean, fresh, low gravity environment which will undoubtedly be the base of most commercial mining and transport, due to its proximity to Earth and content of materials like Helium-3 and even water ice. The Moon will also possibly act as a spaceport to asteroid mining operations and even Mars colonization.

While rockets can be launched from the Moon easily they are still using consumable fuels. The need to use materials and weight to get something from the surface to orbit or vice versa is a waste. Rockets also break down easily, and are limited to a frequency of travel based on refueling operations and repairs. A space elevator has the potential to run off a clear view of the sun, is a simple machine, compared to a rocket, and is able to work 24-7 going up and down. Not to mention the fact that it is a fixed point of operations. It will always be in the same place ensuring there is no danger of missing a landing pad and hitting a habitat.

The construction of a space elevator is not as simple as just landing rockets, however. The basic idea is to anchor a cable to the surface of the moon. That cable is then strung, from the surface, several thousand miles to a weight. This weight keeps the cable tight. It is similar to if you held a string with a ball on the end and then spun around. An elevator car can then run along the cable to and from orbit. All of this is possible with the materials available today. And while the set-up is risky and stringing several thousand miles of cable straight up from the Moon will be expensive, once established the elevator has little potential for problems afterward. And the cost to operate such a structure would be fixed over its lifetime just as the railroads are.

The economic benefits of a space elevator, once built on the Moon are enormous. Landing of scientific payloads would be faster and more reliable, since organizations would not have to develop landers, unless exploring other areas of the Moon. The elevator would allow for the creation of a space dock. This would be an area were spaceships would stop to unload and refuel while passengers and materials are moved to and from the Moon by the elevator.

Essentially the group that owns the elevator would own the only bridge to the Moon. It would be in the same situation as the early railroads. A colony would grow around it and all commerce would move through it. That will be an important consideration when finding a location for such a structure.

As a business it could begin by simply offering transport to the surface at a reduced cost and increased reliability to building a lander. But as time goes on it could just be a toll elevator. A fixed cost transport one direction or the other, though seasonal costs will likely be a factor. Such seasons would be determined by activities like tourism or launch frequency based on Earth weather.

The business danger to this system is similar to the railroads. If it doesn't run there is still the fixed costs of maintaining the system. Though we would hazard a guess that those costs would be minimal. Since the elevator comes into contact with nothing other than the vacuum of space environmental wear will be low. If used heavily enough it will require component maintenance but when that occurs the business will still be cash flow positive.

If the elevator were built tomorrow the real business challenge would be paying off the upfront construction cost in a timely manner while the industry catches up. Lunar mining will likely be the best solution since it can be performed autonomously and continuously. LiftPort is going this direction.

LiftPort is moving to build a lunar space elevator by 2020. The organization raised $100,000 on Kickstarter in 2014 to continue development of their design. They are intending to use a Kevlar ribbon as the main cable of the elevator, which is the most vital and difficult component of the system. The elevator is meant to cart lunar samples into orbit.

At this point LiftPort hasn't stated what the cost of construction would be. Though with possible launch costs and material cost it will undoubtedly be in the fractions of billions of dollars. If they succeed they will set a valuable precedent about the feasibility of the technology.

The space elevator continually appears in media as a technology to replace rockets on Earth. Unfortunately, there are just to many practical problems with such devices on our planet at this time. But space elevators are a very good idea in the correct areas. They are easy to operate, once built, and do replace rocket technologies with something more reliable. And while we have said many technologies will be valuable as businesses in the private space industry, lunar space elevators will likely be the most likely to succeed. Their superiority to conventional space transport is unrivaled from a technological and business standpoint. If a space elevator is built on the Moon those who own it will control much of the industry in that area. No one will swim a river when they can cross a bridge.

Note: For more detailed information of space elevators see this NASA report on the technology: The Space Elevator by Bradley Edwards Ph.D.

Mars

Interplanetary Communications Company

    As the space industry begins to look beyond Earth orbit, communications systems better than those currently used will need to be implemented.

    Let's focus entirely on communication with Mars. This is the target planet for most manned missions and the Moon is able to communicate directly with Earth without special systems.

    In order to communicate effectively with Mars there are a couple issues that must be overcome. One is the six minute time-lag caused by the distance to Mars. The other is the fact that signals are periodically blocked by either the planets or the sun moving in front of the communication satellites.

    The second problem is the simplest to solve. It just requires more satellites. Perhaps two around each planet so that the signal is never hidden when the satellite goes behind the body. At least two would have to be built around the sun for the same reason. Mars One is utilizing a system like this for its communication with the colony it intends to establish. But they will only be using three satellites. One around each planet and then the sun. This system will ensure that there are only a few two hour periods of blackout when a planet is in the way as well as two week periods when the sun gets in the way.

    While the system is effective, for a limited mission, it is not ideal as the colony grows and activity increases. Two weeks of blackout will not be acceptable.

    A problem of bandwidth will also arise, with increased traffic. This problem will require multiple satellites in order to transfer information quickly and reliably enough.

    Eventually a network of dozens of satellites around the sun and each planet will have to be created to ensure optimized 24/7/365 communication between the bodies.

    Then comes the issue of time lag between planets. Relativity stops us from overcoming this problem with available technology. Currently, there is no way to have a live conversation effectively between Earth and Mars. So ways of creating the illusion of instant connectivity will have to be created.

Again using Mars One as an example. They intend to allow astronauts to download websites to a colony server to browse on a regular basis. All this requires is a periodic data-dump to the colony with a copy of your Facebook feed from 4 hours before.

The trouble with this system is that it requires a server in the colony, taking up weight and space. If a single company was maintaining the "phone network" then satellites around Mars could be outfitted with local servers just for the purpose of storing information. This would not only reduce the requirements on each new Mars mission to integrate local servers in place of food, but also allows for Mars to develop an information independence of Earth as it grows. Such a system would ensure that Mars would have a completely formed information infrastructure that anyone on the planet could access without having to build it themselves.

Now this is an audacious goal, one which would take perhaps decades to implement but it can begin now. A space communications company can be created which could initially be profitable be serving as the communications hub for NASA research missions as well as potential manned missions. If someone moved quickly enough they could be contracted by Mars One to build and launch a system in the next five years.

It might not even be necessary to build everything from scratch and launch it. If the budget is really tight, it might be possible for a company to purchase existing Mars satellites that are considered obsolete, then refurbish them remotely to become an effective communications network, limited though they may be.

Such a communication entity would ensure that systems are standardized for all missions since agencies and companies will not want to develop their own communications systems when they can simply piggy-back an existing one.

The business model for a space communications company would most likely be one of a basic data plan. How many gigabits does the organization want to send across the network? OK. They cost this much. This has worked well terrestrially and there is no reason to think that it wouldn't in space.

It has been mentioned how an interplanetary communications company will eventually change into a planetary communications company just by being the foundational network for a new world. But there is one other aspect as well. As individuals and companies begin to truly go out into space to explore, prospect, colonize it will still be necessary to communicate with home. But the same limitations apply, lag and bandwidth. A series of satellites set up to aide communication between Earth and Mars would also become a hub for all space communications. Whether they be from the asteroid belt, Jupiter, or Venus. The network created to communicate with Mars would become the network used to communicate with everything else. It would basically be the telephone booths and operators of space. That is a successful business. Becoming the primary information carrier.

Companies such as SpaceX obviously realize this potential. SpaceX recently announced partnering with Google and Fidelity to create a space-based internet service for Earth. This is just a stepping stone, to pay the bills, until Elon Musk, the CEO of SpaceX, can create the connection with Mars.

Martian Culture

Mars will likely be the first planet, after Earth, which humans will have a permanent presence upon. But what will a Martian society be like? How will it develop and what will Martians be like to trade with. What will be the state of technology. And what will be the mindset of a Martian. In order to create a multiplanetary economy these are all questions that must be explored.

Here are the basic predictions we'll cover in this post. Mars will be agrarian. It will be technologically advanced initially. Martians will be highly independent. Mars will be an ecological experiment station. It will lead advances in agriculture and genetics. It will be a planetary country. Any commerce, at the beginning, on Mars will be basic bartering and trading.

To imagine Mars will be agrarian is a given. In order to survive initial colonist will be required to have a firm grasp of agriculture. This will continue for perhaps hundreds of years as farming is the only means to produce the food needed on Mars. It will remain the focus until Mars is terraformed.

In the early days the farming will occupy the attention of many of the people in a colony. The limited space and inhospitable environment will require constant attention be given to farms to ensure they produce adequately. Automation and robotics will likely come to replace the amount of attention and labor given to day to day farming activities. However, the farm will remain the primary focus of the colonists. Therefore when they gain time for research and study it will be toward methods of improving the farming techniques to increase their standard of living

While Martian society will be based on agriculture the society will still be technologically advanced. In order to land and then live on Mars for any period of time requires technologies which are not commonplace on Earth. There will be a dependency of Martian society on that technology. And, in order to grow at an appreciable rate the best and newest technologies will have to be delivered. Not to mention the fact that genetics and material science will be important aspects of Martian survival based on the farming foundation. Both of those fields require highly advanced technology. But since exploitation of Martian resources to produce such products as silicon chips will be difficult, Earth will have to supply it. Technology will be the Earth's primary export to Mars.

In fact, as compared to Earth the technological infrastructure of Mars will be greater. This will be a side effect of establishing a colony on Mars. Anything that does not have to be landed will not be landed. For this reason communications will be wireless from the very beginning and computing will likely be in the form of orbital data centers. Such a system simplifies the delivery of such technological payloads from Earth.

Concerning power generation. Mars will begin using solar and nuclear power sources. Coal and other fossil fuels will not be an option. This will again leap ahead of Earth. Perhaps to such an extent that even orbital power plants will be in use early in the society due to the access to Earth delivery craft. Nuclear will be an option since fears of such technology will not exist on Mars.

To explain why such technologies as nuclear reactors will not be feared on Mars we should discuss the people. To be blunt Martians will be the best people alive. Mars is too far away and too expensive to send herds of people to. Even if a launch from Earth becomes inexpensive the cost and risk of landing large groups of people on the planet are too great. So with fewer people being delivered they will be sifted.

Unlike the Americas Mars has few initial resources to draw from. The people that are sent to Mars will have to be geneticists, botanists, and farmers who are able to adapt Earth ecology to the Martian environment quickly and without hesitation. When we say "farmers" that is exactly what we mean. Not some professor of agriculture but a farmer who has been able to make horrible ground yield a crop. Practical experience will be essential to all Martian settlers. When creating a colony intellectual pursuits will have to be focused toward practical decisions and action.

Now, since all of the people that are chosen to become Martian colonists will be practical and scientific individuals they will not have a mindset obscured by propaganda. Fears of meltdowns and the like, which inhibit nuclear power on Earth, will be ignored by Martians who have no such luxury as fear when there are only a few options that will work for them.

This practicality and intellectual aptitude, which will grow in Martians, will make them highly independent. Perhaps even more independent than the Americas were. The continual need for survival, little chance of return, and a far greater lack of resources than in the Americas will force Martians to depend on no one but each other.

Martians will have to be very tolerant as well. To be cooped up together for long periods of time will require it. Even as colonies grow into enclosed cities all Martians will be in close proximity to each other.

The colonies will also likely be only one single colony. It makes no sense to attempt to colonize a planet with multiple small settlements. The foundational work and infrastructure is too great. Earth's international affairs will likely move far enough along that only a single colony will ever be attempted, supported by all parties involved. This raises the diversity line again. The colony will have to adopt a single language and societal structure which will span all the cultures that will arrive. This commonality will be helped along by the practicality inherent in early Martians.

From this single colony Martian society will grow. Since multiple colonies will not be pursued multiple Martian cultures will not arise early on. This will create a single Martian society. Unlike Earth, Mars will not be a planet filled with countries; it will be a planet-country. Certainly, if Mars is ever terraformed then cultures and customs may come to vary just as they do when you move from a farm to a city on Earth. But the governmental, economic, and societal structure will be unified over the entire planet.

The economic structure of Mars will be long based on trading and bartering. Trade some carrots for some cabbage, or a potato for some water. The need to survive again working. As a Martian city arrives and not everyone is working to survive then currency will arrive. It will be digital from the very beginning. Mars will never adopt any kind of paper money. The technological aspect of Martian society will never require hard physical money.

Now, the biggest question is how Mars will trade and interact with Earth. Earth will be holding the leash of Mars for some time. Earth will provide the capital, technology, and transportation from the get-go.

As far as how much control Earth will exercise over Mars, it will be nominal. The only organizations to send colonies to Mars initially will be governments and non-profits. Even today much of the Mars movement is coming from foundations, and even Mars One will likely not turn a large profit. There is little commercial value in Mars.

But since those Earth organizations working to establish human presences on Mars are doing it for the sake of doing it they will not have any interest in the colony once it is established. While Britain wished to control the American colonies due to the value of it natural resources and taxes from residents, Mars will have no such resources since its population won't be able to grow as quickly as America did and it has no significant resources.

Once Martian society is established it will have one principle export. Its knowledge and technologies developed for agriculture. Mars will be a hotbed of agricultural and ecological innovation. Experiments and advances will be made due to lack of regulation and danger of negative affects to the barren environment. These advances will be needed on Earth as its population continues to grow. The need for more efficient food production and possibilities of climate control are all problems that will be tackled on Mars.

The great aspect of all of these technologies is that they are not material. They will not be hard goods but information. Information and knowledge can be transported very cheaply from Mars. It requires no rocket fuel just a little electricity. Martian exports will be the genetic designs and agricultural technology which allows that society to flourish on a planet ill-suited for it.

So to sum up. Mars will be a technologically advanced agrarian society which will be fiercely independent of Earth. Its citizens will have a myriad of backgrounds but will all be extremely talented and practical. Mars will form a planetary country and will trade agricultural advances with Earth for technological supplies.

This discussion and theorizing could turn into a book very easily. We have only done a poor job of scraping the surface of what a potential Martian society would be and much of it may never come to pass. But as the reality of a Martian society comes into view these topics will be important.

Note: To read more about Martian trade possibilities read "The Economic Viability of Mars Colonization" by Robert Zubrin

Space Bioengineering

Space is a new environment. A clean slate. As far as we know devoid of even simple life. A new environment where living creatures have never prospered requires new creatures that have never existed. While machines are being developed to take people and other machines into space, organisms need to be developed to allow us to stay there and build an economy and society.

DARPA has already begun exploring the possibilities of genetically modified or synthetically created organisms with which to terraform Mars. However the creation of genetically modified animals has any number of other applications. Plants with increased oxygen producing ability. Bacteria for breaking down asteroids. Modified food producing organisms for colonies. Organisms that can convert human waste into bioluminescent light instead of using electricity. And even bacteria which could solve health hazards to humans caused by radiation or low gravity.

The reason genetic engineering has not been widely accepted and experiences great resistance on Earth is the fact that genetic engineering is considered unnatural. To introduce a man-made plant or organism into the Earth ecosystem is generally considered dangerous due to the side-effects that may arise. An example could be that weeds can adopt a genetically engineered resistance to common herbicides. Or that genetically modified food has detrimental health effects.

These potential problems with genetically engineered organisms is due to their foreignness to the normal ecosystem. Something which evolves 200 years in one or two affects its competition and consumers in ways not anticipated. It is the reaction of the environment which causes opposition to genetic modification not the modified species themselves.

Another argument to genetic modification has been the ethical question of if humans should exercise such powers. This is a question that cannot be answered in this essay. Though, as a guess, this question is still based on the protection of the natural environment.

In space there is no natural environment. It is a microwaved wasteland with no biology. For this reason many of the arguments for using biologically or synthetically engineered organisms fall apart. There is not an ecosystem to ruin with the introduction of a designed-for-space organism.

However, there will still be resistance to the use of such organisms. This is something which space bio-engineering firms will have to be prepared for. Just as deserts and forests are preserved from irrigation or clearing to preserve their natural beauty, so to may barren planets be defended from terraformation. This is a legal question which will have to be addressed in future as such applications as terraformation go from theory to fact.

Also, while at the moment introduction of genetically modified organisms may be acceptable in space, the industry must be careful in future to ensure that created ecosystems are kept clear of dangerous or invasive species.

From a business perspective bioengineering could be comparable to any other human space product in market size, perhaps even larger as terraformation becomes a possibility. But on the smaller scale humans, being natural creatures, require natural solutions to space survival. A typical technological carbon scrubber on a space station in not as effective or efficient as a common plant. But rare is the plant that collects high volumes of CO_2 and can flourish in the low temperatures of Mars.

Not only are new organisms needed for space, they are required. The new environments are so foreign to anything that exists on Earth that finding an existing species to perform some task may be nearly impossible (excluding bacteria that can survive in space while in hibernation). Selective breeding and cross breeding would be far to slow. Just as one has to leap a hundred miles straight up to reach space so must organic life "leap" in survival skills and production to survive in space. Genetic engineering is the only method available to make that leap.

Asteroids and Beyond

Space Surveyor

Asteroid mining will become an integral part of the future space industry. Asteroids contain the vital water, precious metals, and raw materials for space companies to profit from and build with. But how does a future space miner know which asteroids could contain the mother lode? They don't. At this point one rock is as good as another. But a company could be created whose sole purpose would be to explore asteroids and become "the space surveyor" whose product is information.

There are several ways a business for space surveying could be executed. It could create a network of Earth-based telescopes that search for asteroids with certain sizes and orbits. It could create orbital telescopes that also look at size and orbit, but could see more and even do some basic spectrography on the rocks to determine composition. And last, actual exploratory spacecraft can be created that go map and collect samples of asteroids.

A far as a profit strategy goes, the company would be in the business of selling information. It would provide data on all of the objects that it has explored. This data could be maps, locations, compositions, etc. In return for this information, the surveying company could receive either a base fee or a piece of the profits that the mining company receives. With this strategy the surveying company would have very little risk and would be able to focus completely on developing better exploratory technologies.

If anyone doubts the feasibility of this idea they should know that one company is actually, already working towards all of the above concepts in an iterative process. Planetary Resources, is just completing the creation of an orbital asteroid surveying telescope that is small and inexpensive. The purpose of these telescopes will be to map as many near-Earth asteroids as possible. Then P.R. is going to create surveying spacecraft that explore the asteroids that they find with the telescopes. Once that is complete, they intend to create the actual mining craft that will collect the asteroids and move them to where they need to go, like space stations, colonies, or lunar orbit.

The trouble with this model is that Planetary Resources is trying to do everything themselves. They are trying to take on all of the development, deployment and management, of both the discovery and the mining of the asteroids. If they were to focus on just finding ideal candidates for mining, Planetary Resources would be able to become "the company" to get information on viable asteroids to mine. With that being said, P.R. has been leveraging all kinds of income streams from their work so far, so it will not be surprising if they back off on their ambitions of mining in order to become the information company envisioned in this article.

Exploration will always be a part of the space industry. But as more companies look to the possibilities of space they will come to realize that it is much easier to ask for help than to "do it yourself." The space surveying companies that are being created now and in the future will be the "trail guides" of the new frontier. Telling the noobs where the best places to search for the gold is, for a price.

The Space Holodeck

Extended time spent in space can have any number of psychological effects on space crews. Being locked inside a metal can with absolutely nothing outside and no one to help if there is a problem will wear on anyone. Not to mention the endless boredom and routine. While a spaceship will need constant supervision there will never be enough to do during a 2-3 year mission to Mars and back. Crews will need some form of entertainment. But not just movies and books. The crews of long duration spaceflights need something to connect them with home. Something that will give them a reprieve from the isolation of space. Luckily, movie-makers and futurists have already created such a device. The Holodeck.

The "Holodeck" of science fiction is a virtual reality (VR) room that becomes completely interactive. The user becomes a part of a different world , which they can see and interact with using all of their senses. In science fiction the holodeck experience is accomplished through "hard light." No such technology exists today. However limited virtual reality is starting to gain significant traction in the video game industry and a little in the film industry. Products like the Kinect and the Oculus Rift insert the player into the game they are playing. The Oculus Rift creates the illusion of being in the game through a pair of video goggles that let the user see the environment of the game as if through the eyes of their character. They move their head to the left they see the left and vice-versa. Goggles like the Rift can also be interfaced with treadmills and devices, like the Kinect, that track the users body movements. This allows the user of these complete systems to interact with the game using their entire body, running, jumping, and shooting just as if they were actually in the world. But these systems currently only let the user interact with the game and not the game with the user. Players can't feel the recoil of a gun or smell the smoke, they can only move around in it. And yet that may be all that is needed for space.

While the VR systems of today are designed for gaming they could easily be turned into a means of remaining connected with Earth. Complete systems that include a treadmill, goggles, and sensors could be installed on future spaceships. Then, when astronauts go for a jog, instead of simply looking at a wall while they run on the treadmill, they can put on the goggles and immediately be transported to the edge of the Grand Canyon. They would be able to see the sunrise and, for just a little while, feel as if they have the entire Earth underfoot instead of being thousands of miles away from it. This can have tremendously positive effects on the crew.

A company that would want to pursue this type of technology would need to develop two things. First they would need to create a complete VR system that tracks the user and lets them interact with their environment. This has already been accomplished, so most of the focus would be on the second part. Creating the virtual environments from video gathered on Earth.

The company would need to create a means to make a video, of say a jog along the Grand Canyon, interactive. The user of the video would need to be able to "stop and smell the roses" without having to pause the video. This will require a means of layering panoramic video from multiple cameras and syncing it perfectly. This hasn't been accomplished in the VR industry yet. The standard graphics for VR today are mostly CGI because it is easier to create a VR environment within a fake world. But they look clunky and plastic. While these would have their place in entertainment for future space travelers, they would not have remotely the same effect as a true interactive image of home.

However, it is possible that, in creating these interactive environments that can't be touched or smelled, the experience could create the reverse of hope. It could bring about desperation from seeing something so real and not being able to feel it. It could be the equivalent of seeing a mirage of water when you are thirsting in the desert. There are too few studies available today to know what kind of effects this technology would have. A company interested in space applications would need to explore the affects thoroughly once created.

The major benefit to a company that creates these future space "holodecks" is that they would be a company that is not limited to the space industry. Many people on Earth want to have the visual experience of a jog on a beach in Madrid or along the Grand Canyon, instead of watching the morning news on their treadmill. And there would be no psychological implications from this type of technology in this situation. It would become a perfect example of advancing terrestrial life while developing products for space.

The company to create a viable environment that really becomes believable, though untouchable, will be one of the leaders of the future VR market. But it may also be able to solve half of the psychological problems associated with the long term isolation associated with current interplanetary spaceflight.

Note: Since this article was written multiple cameras and software programs have been created which make the creation of VR video much easier.

Asteroid Mining

Asteroid mining concerns the finding and then mining of any of the rocks which float around in the void.

In order to be successful, a mining company in space has to do just what a mining company on Earth does. They have to prospect for potential mother loads. Then figure out how to extract the materials they want. And finally, transport all of that material to someone who will buy it to build a space station or a cellphone.

Several companies are already working toward the goal of exploiting the resources which are available in space. Planetary Resources in near to launching their first asteroid tracking satellites and Deep Space Industries is developing technologies which will allow humans to refine and use the materials mined from the asteroids.

Mining has always been one of the main reasons for going to space. The vacuum above our atmosphere is not as empty as many believe. An abundance of raw materials float aimlessly in space. Approximately 37,000-89,000 tons of these rocks fall to Earth each year. The value of asteroids comes from the fact that many of them are expected to contain quantities of rare earth metals, such as platinum, as well as basic elements like iron and sources of water.

Planetary Resources is currently focusing on the rare earth metals that asteroids could supply to Earth markets.

However, many critic mining companies who are going for the rare materials which appear to be abundant in asteroids. The traditional argument is that as soon as a company creates a steady supply of the materials to the Earth then the market will become saturated, prices will drop, and the ability to finance the expensive space missions will disappear.

While this argument is legitimate to a point (if gold were common it would not be valuable) it is short-sighted.

First, rare earth materials like platinum will be in high demand for some time no matter how large the supply is. Materials like platinum have untold untapped potential. The demand would grow if it were possible to work with pounds, instead of grams, of the metal and its cousins.

Secondly, companies like PR are nowhere near to creating a supply that will saturate the market. Within ten years they might be able to retrieve an asteroid the size of a basketball.

When space mining companies do grow they will quickly grow out of the need to rely on Earth-based markets to pay the bills. Once the infrastructure is set up, these companies will be the ones to provide the water and raw materials to build space stations and colonies. The prime technology behind DSI is their zero-gravity 3-D printing technology which will allow them to turn rock and raw iron from an asteroid into a beam or plate or someday a rocket nozzle.

And concerning the inability to pay for expensive missions with the profits from mineral returns, which assumes that space launches and missions will remain expensive. This is clearly not the case seeing that space launch companies like SpaceX have already dramatically reduced the cost of launch and are continuing to do so.

In reality asteroid mining has far fewer market obstacles than many of the other space ventures being pursued.

Unlike the space launch industry, there is currently more than enough demand for the materials space mining companies intend to deliver. And that demand is not within the space industry but across many, ranging from battery manufacturing to catalytic converters.

Mining companies also have an unlimited growth potential, however far into the future you look. No matter how technology changes the raw materials will always need to be collected to build the stuff.

Space mining is a great industry to be on the ground floor of right now because the demand is there and the possibilities are many. The only problem a fresh entrepreneur may have getting into the race is the cost of creating the technology to deliver the goods. Even though PR and DSI are using off-the-shelf components and micro-vehicles they are still not cheap companies.

But, if someone in a garage would like to contribute to space mining there are some technologies which could be pursued quite easily.

Currently there is no definitive way to securely land a craft on small space body. The lack of gravity makes it almost impossible to just set down on the surface. Stemming from this problem is the problem of grabbing a rock and putting it in tow. And then once the asteroid is secured tools and techniques for actually mining it in space are still on the drawing board. Any of these problems are hardware and even software problems which can be pursued and solved on a shoelace budget and a little clever design.

Asteroid mining is happening. True, it is only in its early stages but there always has to be the first prospector to go to California and find the first nugget. Asteroid mining will be one of the foundations of the future space economy. The infrastructure it creates, information it gathers, and the materials it refines will support nearly every other aspect of space travel, colonization, and commercialization.

Law and Order

Space Historical Site Protection and Preservation

As tourists and colonists begin to move out into the solar system they will begin to visit the historical landing sites of Apollo, Luna II, and Curiosity. But who will protect these sites from overambitious souvenir hunters? That is a big question and an opportunity for the future space industry.

Organizations/Companies can and need to be created in order to protect and preserve these sites that are a part of human history. The opportunity comes from either being contracted by governments to "defend" them from vandalism or by turning them into "pay to enter" museums. But the combination of the two will be the most likely. Governments wanting to preserve the artifacts will subsidize any company with the technology to do so. Then the company will be able to charge admission to the site which they have been given protective custody over.

What would be needed to create these museums? Not a lot. On the Moon a simple fence could be erected around the Apollo modules and basically patrolled by robots. Visitors would be able to walk through an automatic system in order to gain access and would be given a tour, probably along a special visitor path to prevent footprints, by a telepresence robot controlled from Earth. The admission fees would be on the order of several thousand dollars in the early days and would come down as lunar travel became more common. All of this would be able to be constructed with rovers, but if lunar tourism is common it would most likely be easier to simply send a human crew to create the site.

On Mars it will be very different. Historical sites will need to be protected from the environment as well as the visitors and there is no chance of telepresence due to radio lag. Each site would need to have a structure built around it, most likely some type of inflatable dome. Or perhaps a solid display case, of sorts, could be created that allows guests to look inside to see the landers but not touch or vandalize them. Another option, since there is no need to preserve footprints on Mars and there are no significantly large structures, a museum could be created and then each of the artifacts would be collected and put on display as in a normal museum on Earth. Again government subsidies would play a large role and then the museum would be able to become one of the "attractions" of a Martian vacation.

But there is no reason to leave all of these artifacts on the Moon or Mars. A time will come when some artifacts may be brought back to their home planet just as pottery is brought from an archaeological dig. Sojourner would be something akin to a famous painting. And the organization that has custody of it will be the one to profit from its transport.

While the first few hundred humans will no doubt be very respectful of the pieces of history that are scattered around the solar system, preservation is an issue that will need to be addressed as space travel and tourism begin to become common. The footprints on the Moon are as irreplaceable as the Mona Lisa. An opportunity exists today for space entrepreneurs to create a framework to protect these artifacts and become the curators and owners of the first interplanetary museums.

The Danger of E.T.

Aliens are bad for business.
No, I don't mean that there will be little green men working to destroy us commercially. In fact, I mean something as basic as a single celled organism could bring the current space industry and prospects of settlement to a halt.
Let me paint a picture for you.
The single largest discovery that could both spark great interest in space but also bring colonization to a standstill would be the discovery

of extraterrestrial life in our solar system. Or even the remains of such life.

This is where space colonization differs completely from all historical explorers. In the past, as colonists and explorers spread across the New World they contaminated it with their diseases and, in some ways, their cultures. It is known that the Americas were once home to millions that were never observed because they were destroyed by European plagues. The potential discoveries were destroyed before they could be discovered. This is what is feared may happen in space by space environmentalists.

Mars and Europa are among the primary targets for space life hunters. They both are expected to have significant enough amounts of water and friendly enough environments to have once or still harbor life. The problem is that these characteristics are also what make those locations prime colonization prospects. But what would happen if either fossils or living samples of life existed on one of those bodies. In our environmentally conscious world, they would be cordoned off as preserves. The E.T.'s would have to be kept separate from all other biological life so that it could not be contaminated by Earth life. This would require that no colony could exist anywhere near the discovery.

So if life were to be discovered on Mars it could stop all Mars exploration for close to fifty years. Because instead of sending missions to colonize and then study, missions would be sent to study and then possibly colonize. The danger of destroying or contaminating either the E.T. or ourselves would entice Earth governments to stop human transport.

Now, what is truly disturbing about this condition is that an E.T. could be discovered that originated on Earth. Right now there are numerous rovers on Mars. And even though they have been cooked and sterilized they still could have carried to the planet microbes that could survive if they were exposed to the right conditions. Now suppose that another rover came along behind one of those

dirty rovers. And low and behold that rover finds
microbial life that the other rover "missed." But
the new rover cannot recognize it as an Earth-based
contamination. At this point, having found E.T. on
Mars, the planet is locked down and only particular
scientific missions are arranged. After about ten
years a sample of the organism is brought back to
Earth by robotic rover. By that point the microbes
may have evolved enough to adapt to the Martian
environment. While they will still appear similar to
Earth bacteria, it will continually be questioned
whether they could just have been seeded by an Earth
rock on Mars or vice-versa. And there would be no
way to prove that the rover planted it. Because by
that time, the bacteria could have spread across all
of Mars.

Now Mars has life, of sorts, and the decision has
to be made if we will allow humans to
colonize/continue to colonize the planet, and
introduce all kinds of new biological systems, or
simply keep it as a preserve in honor of the first
place outside of Earth to contain life.

So basically, we may create the E.T. by
delivering infested spacecraft, but then decide that
it was indigenous to the planet and attempt to
protect it by stopping future exploration. Not an
ideal future for a new and growing industry.

While this scenario is fictional, it is still
something that is incredibly possible.

At the current rate of planetary bio-research it
appears that many Mars launches and colonies will be
established before any type of life is discovered,
if ever. So, if perchance, the organism is
legitimately alien, a human colony will most likely
have to be one of the means of studying it. So
instead of stopping colonization such discoveries
may simply limit ideas of terraforming or expansion
of colonies. It will really come down to a question
of how much of the planet should be preserved or if
it is even possible to. More or less it will be a
system just like that of the United States with its
parks and preserves.

As the industry grows detection and preservation of possible E.T. locations will have to be consciously considered. Something that was lacking in much past exploration of our globe. But all preservation will need to be conducted in a way that is beneficial it the people that are risking their lives and fortunes to open the gates of space. Preservation on Earth has led to the devastation of several industries where the protection was taken too far.

Now the fear of certain parts of space being restricted due to biological contaminations may not be an issue at all for several decades. Since many governments today are relatively Earth-bound there is no means for them to prohibit colonization except to prohibit Mars-bound launches. And if one country grounds launches to Mars another may not. So policing of bio-contamination would have to be a uni-world decision. Something that is unprecedented.

There is also the question of when a life form no longer becomes "from Earth." In the case of a false positive mentioned earlier, organisms that live on Mars for any period of time will evolve to match that environment. There will come a time when new species will have to classified that only exist on certain planets. New rules will have to be created to determine when a species that originated on Earth but now can only live on Mars requires special attention or protection.

Overall, the possibility of bio-contamination is much more of a legal hypothetical than a business opportunity, except that is for the burgeoning space-lawyer and legislator.

To see more visit the NASA page for the Office of Planetary Protection. It discusses means the organization uses to prevent forward contamination of planets with Earth organisms.

Space Crime

Crime follows wherever there is either want or money. Space will have both. It will begin as disputes over needed resources and will likely develop into full blown space pirates that could endanger ships.

In the early days of space there will be a few primary resources that everyone will need. These include water, fuel, and energy. These things will be the gold of space for many years. Space farers will trade these as they would currency. It will be a system identical to the old west trading posts. The trouble is, there will eventually be those that have nothing to trade. An asteroid ship that is out of fuel and has found no rocks with water to barter.

In the very beginning there will no doubt be a space "code of conduct" where people simply help themselves out because they know they all need it. It will be a "do unto others" mentality, brought on by the greater purpose of space colonization. But eventually that will likely fade. Those that are in need may be ignored in order to gain a higher profit. This will be when the crime begins. Space farers will begin to steal from each other either to survive or to make a buck. Again, as in the old west, one could steal a man's gold or his canteen. In space these will be one and the same, at the start. This will be the beginning of crime. Taking the resources of others in order to satisfy an assumed need. Meeting a quota, going farther, or staving off thirst.

Later space will develop to where these basic needs will be able to be fulfilled easily. This is the point where space is no longer a frontier and is rather a fully developed economy. Ships no longer look for the bare necessities. They instead look for profit. Ships will transport precious metals, large supplies of water, or passengers. These become the target of true criminals that are not hunting out of necessity but out of greed.

In space it is nearly impossible to intercept another ship by chance; there is just too much space. So the old means of just floating around until something comes along will not be what happens. However, the space culture will have several characteristics that will be of help to criminals. One, all ships will be able to contact each other and likely be tracked by some form of ground control. This information will be vulnerable to hacks, leading pirate ships to cargo ships filled with platinum asteroids. Second, even if pirates can't find ships in open space they will be able to lay in wait at major ports. Such as in orbit around the Moon and Mars. This makes it less difficult to organize targets.

In the case of waiting in orbit for a target. It will be possible because criminals will likely arrive before security services. This will change as space body guards and space police become established in order to protect the ships in port or even in transit.

As far as crime goes I have only truly spoken about theft. There are other facets that could be discussed but that would make this essay go on forever. Therefore, those skews of the topic will be saved for future discussion.

Really, the best analogy for what space will be like, concerning crime, as it develops, is the Wild West. People will kill for your gold, steal your horse, take your pick, drink your water, and anything else you can think of. And it will remain like this until countermeasures are created.

Space is just a huge frontier that will require a much more developed and even multiplanetary society to maintain any kind of law enforcement or protection. When spacecraft come down to the cost of a large boat today, crime will become as commonplace as we see today in normal life. It will, primarily, be the responsibility of the prospectors and the explorers of space to find the means of protecting themselves as they go about their lives.

Space Body Guards

When space becomes a true society and economy space crime will develop. There will be dangers from pirates, rogue groups, and governments raiding cargo ships, and even small explorers, for precious metals or resources. Ships that are prospecting or carrying any type of precious cargo (human or inanimate) will likely need some protection. The development of space "body guards" will be necessary.

These personal protectors will be able to take many shapes. Robotic or manned. Integrated or separate.

Most likely, such a company will begin by creating small groups of drones that can be rented by ships.

These drones would act as scouts generally, but could be used as killer satellites, ramming other ships, should a ship ever be attacked. By the time such devices are needed AI will have developed enough that remote control will not be necessary. The protectors will be able to behave as a dog would when its owner says "sick'em."

As time goes on manned craft will be developed that will essentially be escort fighters. This would be a very elite type of group probably only contracted by dignitaries or large corporations.

The need for protection of standard cargo and transport ships will decrease as more are launched and used. Therefore, such a security force will quickly become something for the niche market of the very paranoid or the very rich and important, just as private body guards today.

The primary reason that such force will be needed more in the beginning is because the harshness and greed in space will create the same kind of desperate crime that existed during the California Gold Rush. Those in space will need a body guard or guard dog just as the western prospectors once did to protect their claims and supplies.

Certainly, these types of "body guards," manned or unmanned, would require changes to current space

112

law, which prohibit such weapons in space, in order
to exist. But such changes will come about when
those in space need protected as much as the people
on the surface of a planet.

Invasive Species in Space

From time to time one will hear of something
called "invasive species." Invasive species are
organisms which are introduced to an area where they
have no competition and thus begin to roust the
native species and wreak havoc with the ecosystem.
Such species include numerous noxious weeds, fish
such as carp, and animals like pet pythons.

Nearly all of these invasive species were
introduced by human interaction. A seed stuck to a
boat, a pet released into a swamp, etc. All of these
species which began as only one or two loose seeds
have become major problems on our planet and within
many countries as they can destroy what makes a
river, lake, land desirable in a particular area.

It is too late now to point this out as all the
harm has been and is being done now. However there
is no reason to allow it to continue, at least for
some time.

It has been said many times that humans are on
the cusp of an exodus to space. The price of
launches is expected to decrease dramatically in the
coming decades so that a trip into the void could be
within the range of vacation expenses. There are
also plans to begin colonizing Mars. But will the
mistakes of old be overlooked? Will we carry
invasive or undesirable species with us as we move
into space?

NASA and other space agencies have long worked to
ensure that biocontamination does not occur between
its craft and the heavenly bodies they explore. And
yet even with all the scrubbing, baking and
sanitizing that is performed on craft such as
rovers, they have been found to still harbor
microbes which could colonize the Red Planet before

humans. If highly polished equipment is still carrying bacteria, what is expected to occur when people are throwing suitcases into the cargo hold of a spaceship for a vacation? Mosquitoes might be released into what could have been an Eden.

The private space industry is moving quickly to develop technologies for transportation. But as the transit becomes more viable the industry must remember to perform the annoying housecleaning tasks and consider them before history is simply repeated. Invasive species are a large problem on Earth where they have little competition, but they could be devastating to a space mission if resilient bacteria were introduced to a colony's single water supply where there is no competition. Not to mention the potential extraterrestrial conservation issues such an outbreak might incur.

While a cleaning bureaucracy does not need to be created to hinder the industry it is something that should be developed before it is needed. Because when a biological invasion occurs it will appear as gross negligence on the part of the industry. From that will spawn a truly hindering organization.

The industry must work on problems such as invasive species and others which are all preventable. This will show responsibility and due diligence which will give the industry leeway when other unforeseeable problems occur.

As always, this potential cleaning problem opens an opportunity for space entrepreneurs. Currently space rovers are not being cleaned completely. But they are being cleaned as well as they can be. This means that new methods of scrubbing spacecraft need to be developed as well as means of containing microbes and large potential invasive species during manned flights.

Such a business could begin life performing basic cleaning on spacecraft going into orbit. Basically a prepper for low risk launches. Then, as more rovers are deployed and more people move into space, launch companies could solicit the services of such a company to screen passengers and cargo for potential biohazards and invasive species. Some launch companies may elect to do this themselves but until launch reliability is the same as an airplane launch companies will likely not wish to hold the liability for a potential infestation of a space station. A company dedicated to the screening and cleaning of cargo and people could develop the methods and the technologies to keep invasive and dangerous species out of pure areas.

Those who do not learn from history are doomed to repeat it. Weeds, reptiles, germs, fish and many other kinds of creatures have repeatedly been carried into areas where they can wreak havoc and destroy something that was devoid of such organisms. In space, humans have a completely clean slate. We can have any kind of flora or fauna we want. But there must be means of keeping what shouldn't go to space from going to space. A few mosquitoes would completely ruin a trip to a space station.

Seasteading as a Foundation for Space Law

There are several examples in history which can be used to avoid stumbling blocks in the current and coming space economy. Antarctica, America, etc. However, anything that has happened in history is now set in stone and cannot be experimented with only theorized upon. But space is an expensive place to go, experimentation, with technologies, and particularly law, in cheaper settings would be highly useful. Fortunately, there is a place that serves as a viable testing ground of space communities and how they will interact with Earth communities.

Over the last few years there has been a small movement for what is called seasteading. It is all predicated on the idea of creating what amounts to artificial floating cities or countries, on the Earth's oceans. This movement is now lead, primarily, by the Seasteading Institute.

At the introduction of seasteading a book was written to outline challenges to seasteading, some technical others legal. Not surprisingly, many issues discussed in the book will be faced by space communities.

The seas are a legal fuzzy area. While after a certain distance there is technically no jurisdiction countries can still exercise authority for a number of reasons. There are dangers of pirates. Questions exist of whether a floating city can truly define its own laws and standards of conduct. How would an isolated community support itself financially or justify its construction? How does an artificial structure support the biological needs of its inhabitants? All of these issues, which apply to a community in the unclaimed, empty, shifting, blue void, also apply to a community in the unclaimed, empty, shifting black void.

While seasteading is an expensive and risky undertaking it is far less so than the creation of a space station. Movers in the space industry should consider this movement very seriously. Any world decisions made about free, privately-funded entities in international waters would likely be applied to free privately-funded entities in international space.

If such floating cities were created the space industry would be able to explore and even shape the political, social, and financial ramifications of space flight in as close a simulation as is possible. If technologies must be tested and proven so to should the sociological designs. Seasteading can provide this opportunity.

The creation of islands on Earth can define how the islands in the sky will interact with the world they are leaving but still interacting with.

Other Thoughts

Crashes and Accidents

"Space is hard - but worth it" Sir Richard Branson
At the writing of this post the private space industry has suffered two major accidents. A failed launch of an Orbital Sciences Antares Rocket and the crash of SpaceShipTwo during a test flight, which killed one pilot.

These accidents will no doubt have huge detrimental effects to the industry which was just beginning to gain a bright outlook on the future. Public opinion will likely swing back into fear of space as opposed to the wonder of it.

It is important to remember that at this point space is at the same place aviation was after Lindbergh's flight. The technology is proven to get us to the moon. Private companies can make it into space. Now we are all waiting for the space age Boeing 247 to take us to the stars.

But creating a space liner is leaps and bounds more difficult than building an airliner, and that was difficult. There have been and will continue to be accidents as space develops. But we must not let those change the resolve to go to space.

Space is far more than a commercial opportunity. At the moment there is actually very little money in it compared to other industries, due to the expense. Space is a future that only a few really believe in and others fear. The trouble is that those who fear it want to project that fear onto others. And that fear is unfounded because it is like being afraid of the first Russian spacecraft. The fear is of what it is today and not of what it will become tomorrow. They point to the accidents and warn of the dangers which come with space travel though they have never experienced it and don't see that the "now" is not the "future."

The people that died in the accidents were not afraid because they could see what the future held and it excited them. And the only way to truly honor their memory is to continue on towards the goal that they themselves gave their lives believing in.

Any space travel company will have to come face to face with the possibility of the loss of life. But the only thing they can do is work to avoid it as much as possible. Negligence cannot be allowed.

Space travel is more than a half a century old but commercial systems are coming into service. It took aviation 30 years to go from first flight to airliner. Considering the challenges and the cost of space travel we are doing decently well. But fear and accidents cannot be allowed to stop the progress; otherwise it may be delayed decades.

Space companies must be able to take the lessons learned from their mistakes and work to improve. While it may be tragic, fear cannot be allowed to win.

Fortunately fear of progress never wins. As is proven by aviation and any number of other advances. Fear is only able to slow something down but never stop it. Possibilities outweigh fear any day. These accidents may cripple the industry but they will not stop it

But possibilities only become real when they are made real. Space companies and entrepreneurs must learn how to create possibility out of tragedy. By doing this they will be able to progress without so much as a break in step. People may die but they would not want it to be in vain by having their work undermined by the failure of the company or industry that they represented in life. They are the leaders of the space crusade and others must take up their positions.

Space is the future of the human race. What better industry to support and be a part of.

Transporting Nothing

In "The Space Economy" we try to focus on technologies that are either currently feasible or possible in the near future. But, we decided to break it up a little bit and reach a little further out.

What is the fundamental problem facing nearly every space company today, or even in the future. Cost to move or make stuff to and in space. At this moment it costs just under $1000 a pound to transport something into orbit. Cheap enough that private sector companies have greater access, but it is not something that would become really widespread. And even with further reduced launch costs, traditional transport will always be expensive, it is an historical fact.

The industry expects to be able to mine asteroids to provide fuel for ships, and even make the ships out of asteroid concrete. But, construction is expensive, has always been, and as long as it's being built from natural materials, will always be.

Physical "stuff" is the enemy of spaceflight. Now, and even in 50-100 years.

What if it were possible to just get rid of all of it? Just not have mass or materials in spacecraft or habitats or anything else. Space would become something that would be able to grow exponentially since it would cost little to nothing to put stuff in it.

Star Trek had it all right. The ships don't have windows, they have force-fields, no weight. They don't have grapples they have tractor beams, no weight. When people move they use transporters, no transfer of weight, just information. The only thing utilized is controlled energy from the power source that was needed anyway. Imagine how the industry would change if these technologies were available.

Instead of expending millions of dollars to send a person or even materials to the moon or a to a ship in orbit one just calls Scotty and pays a slightly higher electric bill.

Now certainly, not all of this is possible in the near future, but the economic advantages are clear. Transportation and construction of physical things are the bane of the creation of a space organization. Think of a space station. Normally it would he made out of a material, aluminum, Kevlar, etc. If you build a large station in orbit you would likely have a frame and then attach panels to seal it. Instead of building the space station with metal panels what if one used force field generators embedded in the frame. Less labor, less weight to transport, fewer parts to replace, just more power.

Note: Power generation is the bane of any force field. The ISS uses as much power as 55 American homes to stay alive it won't be using a tractor beam. But for this post we'll assume that power technologies have progressed far enough to power energy based mechanics or the systems are made more efficient.

Luckily, some of these ideas are not quite as Sci-Fi as one would expect. Development of a tractor beam has been underway at NASA for several years. And force-field like technologies are used in particle accelerators to help hold the vacuum. These are all technologies that basically create material things form immaterial things. This is what is needed in space since materials are the primary limiting factor in the industry.

A "Hard Light" company could get started today creating devices such as the tractor beam being researched at NASA. They could fund the research by providing micro-versions for private and public asteroid sampling missions where a mechanical system may not be feasible. (Compare a laser pointer to a drill). From there they could work on systems that collect space junk and then push small satellites into higher orbits. There a lot of basic space operations that exist where energy-based manipulation is useful.

Eventually, such a company would be poised to create force fields for habitats and energy based manipulation equipment of all kinds that would be lighter and more durable than any mechanical system. (So what if a micro-meteorite punches a hole in an energy shield. And the tractor beam will probably not get bent.)

Some of the most useful space technologies are still far from feasibility. But, there are places where, in the not too distant future, energy can replace matter, thus replacing the primary expense of space.

Space Robots as Heroes

The space programs of the past and the space industry of the future is subject to public opinion and support. This was true of the moon shots and it is true of each of Apple's unveilings. If people don't care then success is substantially more difficult.

Robots are a great way to explore space. They are cheaper, safer, and faster than humans. And, as artificial intelligence increases they are becoming as capable as a person. So why risk a life if the job can be done by a machine?

Public relations. A machine does not elicit a response from people that makes them stand and root for it. Curiosity landed and continues to provide amazing images and great information but no one, outside of the space community, cares. Voyager is now in interstellar space, no one cares. Opportunity has survived on the red planet for 11 years, no one cares. Sending people to Mars? Great press, though there are now rumors of fraud.

Now certainly humans do need to be in space. Space is there for us, not the machines. But machines are able to blaze trails and provide information in far more effective ways than an astronaut with a wind gauge can. But as entrepreneurs in the space robot business get started how do they work to gain the public support for a Mars rover that is remotely similar to an astronaut?

For this to occur engineers must become showmen. Think of R2-D2, this space robot is loved by millions even over its anthropomorphic partner because R2 is lovable and has a personality. He is just a can that beeps but everyone connects with him. Space robots must become "hims" instead of "its."

So when conducting a scientific or exploratory mission how does one make a "him?" Let's look at another automated space machine that has broken the mold and won the hearts of even average folk, the Hubble Space Telescope. Hubble has gained value as much more than a scientific instrument. This is because it acts as an eye to the universe. It has given the world images of the universe in amazing color. It has a name that people can remember. And it has a story which people relate to. It started broken, was fixed, was almost scrapped, but is still going. Hubble is the little engine that could, and it has survived partially through public support.

Robots and probes must become celebrities in order to have a level of public praise similar to an astronaut. The robot needs to have life on display. It needs to have a story that people can tell. The hurtles that that little circuit board overcame. The more that the machine can be personified the better.

Companies in the space robot industry which are just starting out and need to get through a crowdfunding campaign or have investors hear about them before they walk in the door, need to make their robot a person. Give it a twitter account, an Instagram, maybe spend some weight on a couple of eyeballs. Have the people building it take a personable selfie with it.

Space robots shouldn't be scientific instruments but a friend or adventurer. The humans around the robot can give the robot the life and personality that it needs, but that has to be something that is considered when building it and sending it on its way.

Necessity for Modularity

The cost to enter the space economy is high. It is time, capital, and labor intensive. And yet large corporations and billionaires will not be able to develop the space industry to a point where it is a part of our culture.

With only a few large players in the game there's a limit to how many goals can be scored until everyone is crippled. Even innovative companies like SpaceX will reach a critical mass where they perform only particular duties in the industry. The industry will stagnate unless smaller players can become a part of it.

So what is a strategy that smaller companies and individuals could take in order to make a mark in the space economy?

Let's use a theoretical example, Space-Based Solar Power. This concept for powering the world has been around for decades. The concept of using an unobstructed view of the largest fusion reactor in existence (the sun) for power is very enticing. If space solar power could be implemented then it would solve many of the world's energy problems.

Here is the problem. Space based solar power requires huge initial investment. Basically the lifetime cost of a nuclear power plant is what it would take to build a comparable orbital solar array. This is not a feasible business plan. No matter how great the design or promising the impact 16-20 billion dollars up front is not something people rush to.

So how does one take something hugely expensive and reduce the cost. Break it up into little pieces. Small companies and individuals need to lay out strategies where what they invest in today will still be useful 10 years from now. In this way the cost of something huge can be spread over years and incrementally built. For orbital solar, a specific direction might be to develop something similar to the orbital power plant where the company creates smaller modules to be attached to ships and stations to serve as a temporary power source. When a significant number of cells have been placed in orbit, years from the first, then the modules could be combined with a transmitter to beam the power to Earth instead of to ships.

Modularity has to be the foundation of any small company wishing to build big things. The giant one hit wonder is not feasible. They must find a way to break it down. A Mars colony into single identical modules. A telescope mirror into hundreds of smaller mirrors.

Modularity, building small identical things that can become larger individual things is very scalable and adaptable. If a small company is making habitats for Mars and has simply created a small-tent-like module that connects to others, then the product is as available to a single fanatic as it is to a giant corporation. And the producing company is able to make money from selling one as easily as selling a hundred.

Breaking larger structures down into multiple pieces also decreases the complexity of the design and increases its adaptability. Imagine the difference between having to redo the plumbing of an entire space station or just of the new modules.

Every new private space company is adopting this idea of breaking down the grand dream into individual components that can pay for themselves on a small scale while remaining relevant on the large scale. Bigelow Aerospace is creating, not space stations, but space station modules. Planetary resources is not creating a single advanced asteroid hunting satellite but a swarm of small satellites.

Modularity reduces cost and ensures that a viable product is created more quickly. If anyone is considering creating a space company and they are not a billionaire, they must design the product to be modular and relevant for years. This ensures scalability, adaptability, redundancy, and early returns.

The dreams of launching an entire space station or colony in a few shots can't be done by the entrepreneur in a garage. But sneaking into orbit bit by bit is very feasible. And as launches become ever more common the left over space will be more

available and inexpensive. Space start-ups have to
do more with less until it can all be combined into
a single system

Bibliography

""Dino Killer" Asteroid Was Half the Size Predicted?" *National Geographic*. National Geographic Society. Web. 24 Aug. 2015. <http://news.nationalgeographic.com/news/2008/04/080 410-sea-meteorites.html>.

"...From the Stars We Are Born, to the Stars We Will Return..." *Celestis, Inc*. Web. 24 Aug. 2015. <http://www.celestis.com/>.

"Ablative Armor." *Wikipedia*. Wikimedia Foundation. Web. 24 Aug. 2015. <https://en.wikipedia.org/wiki/Ablative_armor>.

"Alcor's Mission." *Alcor's Mission*. Web. 24 Aug. 2015. <http://www.alcor.org/AboutAlcor/mission.htm>.

"Asian Carp." Web. 24 Aug. 2015. <https://www.nwf.org/Wildlife/Threats-to-Wildlife/Invasive-Species/Asian-Carp.aspx>.

"Astronauts Find Living Organisms Clinging to the International Space Station, and Aren't Sure How They Got There | ExtremeTech." *ExtremeTech*. Web. 24 Aug. 2015. <http://www.extremetech.com/extreme/188479-astronauts-find-living-organisms-clinging-to-the-international-space-station-and-arent-sure-how-they-got-there>.

"Boeing 247." *Wikipedia*. Wikimedia Foundation. Web. 24 Aug. 2015. <https://en.wikipedia.org/wiki/Boeing_247>.

"Canadarm." *Canadian Space Agency Website*. Web. 24 Aug. 2015. <http://www.asc-csa.gc.ca/eng/canadarm/>. "Capabilities & Services." *SpaceX*. Web. 24 Aug. 2015. <http://www.spacex.com/about/capabilities>.

"Chelyabinsk Meteor." *Wikipedia*. Wikimedia
Foundation. Web. 24 Aug. 2015.
<https://en.wikipedia.org/wiki/Chelyabinsk_meteor>.
"Chris Hadfield." *Wikipedia*. Wikimedia Foundation.
Web. 24 Aug. 2015.
<https://en.wikipedia.org/wiki/Chris_Hadfield>.

"Communications System - The Technology - Mars One."
Mars One. Web. 24 Aug. 2015. <http://www.mars-
one.com/technology/communications-system/>.

"Cubesats Explained and Why You Should Build One."
DIY Space Exploration. 30 Mar. 2013. Web. 24 Aug.
2015. <http://www.diyspaceexploration.com/what-are-
cubesats/>.

"DARPA Wants to Genetically Engineer Organisms to
Terraform Mars." *IFLScience*. 26 June 2015. Web. 24
Aug. 2015. <http://www.iflscience.com/space/darpa-
wants-terraform-mars>.

"Development of Space and Pressure Suits | Orbital
Outfitters." *Orbital Outfitters*. Web. 24 Aug. 2015.
<http://orbitaloutfitters.com/about-us/>.
"Dragon." *SpaceX*. Web. 24 Aug. 2015.
<http://www.spacex.com/dragon>.

Dunbar, Brian. "Powering the Future." *NASA*. NASA, 20
Sept. 2011. Web. 24 Aug. 2015.
<http://www.nasa.gov/centers/glenn/about/fs06grc.htm
l>.

"Energy Usage of Server Farms." *Energy Usage of
Server Farms*. Web. 24 Aug. 2015.
<http://large.stanford.edu/courses/2012/ph240/lee1/>

Geuss, Megan. "Google, Fidelity Invest $1 Billion in
SpaceX and Satellite Internet Plan [Updated]." Web.
24 Aug. 2015.
<http://arstechnica.com/business/2015/01/google-
might-pour-money-into-spacex-really-wants-satellite-
internet/>.

"Helium-3." *Wikipedia*. Wikimedia Foundation. Web. 24 Aug. 2015. <https://en.wikipedia.org/wiki/Helium-3>.

"How Stadium Construction Costs Reached the Billions - Athletic Business." *Athletic Business*. Web. 24 Aug. 2015. <http://www.athleticbusiness.com/stadium-arena/how-stadium-construction-costs-reached-the-billions.html>.

"How to Turn Water into Rocket Fuel." *The Independent*. Independent Digital News and Media. Web. 24 Aug. 2015. <http://www.independent.co.uk/news/science/how-to-turn-water-into-rocket-fuel-ndash-scientists-unlock-power-of-the-sun-882613.html>.

"Human Robot Interaction." Web. 24 Aug. 2015. <http://www.cc.gatech.edu/ai/robot-lab/online-publications/sony-iros.pdf>.

"INTERNATIONAL LUNAR OBSERVATORY ASSOCIATION, 4 MISSION UPDATE JANUARY 2014: THE START OF PERMANENT HUMAN OPERATIONS ON THE MOON." *International Lunar Observatory Association*. Web. 24 Aug. 2015. <http://www.iloa.org/4MissionUpdate0114.html>.

"ISEE-3 Reboot Project by Space College, Skycorp, and SpaceRef." *ISEE-3 Reboot Project by Space College, Skycorp, and SpaceRef*. Web. 24 Aug. 2015. <https://www.rockethub.com/42228#description-tab>.

"ISS." *Wikipedia*. Wikimedia Foundation. Web. 24 Aug. 2015. <https://en.wikipedia.org/wiki/International_Space_Station#Cost>.

"If You've Ever Dreamed of Flying, You Can. It's Surprisingly Simple â" but No Less Profound." *Zero Gravity Corporation*. Web. 24 Aug. 2015. <http://www.gozerog.com/>.

"Invasive Pythons." *US News*. U.S.News & World Report. Web. 24 Aug. 2015. <http://www.usnews.com/news/articles/2014/07/21/inva sive-pythons-threaten-florida-everglades>.

"Kinect for Windows." *Kinect for Windows*. Web. 24 Aug. 2015. <http://www.microsoft.com/en-us/kinectforwindows/>.

"Launch Vehicles Then and Now: 50 Years of Evolution." *Launch Vehicles Then and Now: 50 Years of Evolution*. Web. 24 Aug. 2015. <http://www.aerospace.org/2013/12/11/launch-vehicles-then-and-now-50-years-of-evolution/>.

"Lunacrete." *Wikipedia*. Wikimedia Foundation. Web. 24 Aug. 2015. <https://en.wikipedia.org/wiki/Lunarcrete>.

"Lunar Elevator." *LiftPort Group*. Web. 24 Aug. 2015. <http://liftport.com/>.

"Made In Space." *Made In Space*. Web. 24 Aug. 2015. <http://www.madeinspace.us/>.

"Mars One Finalist Announces That It's All A Scam." *IFLScience*. 22 Mar. 2015. Web. 24 Aug. 2015. <http://www.iflscience.com/space/whats-going-mars-one>.

"Michio Kaku on the Space Elevator." *YouTube*. Web. 24 Aug. 2015. <https://youtu.be/sYYdh84pFng>.

"Microbial Stowaways." *Nature.com*. Nature Publishing Group. Web. 24 Aug. 2015. <http://www.nature.com/news/microbial-stowaways-to-mars-identified-1.15249>.

"NASA Developing Real-Life Tractor Beams." *Universe Today*. 3 Nov. 2011. Web. 24 Aug. 2015. <http://www.universetoday.com/90605/nasa-developing-real-life-tractor-beams/>.

"NASA Human Research Program." Web. 24 Aug. 2015. <http://ntrs.nasa.gov/archive/nasa/casi.ntrs.nasa.go v/20100028269.pdf>.

"NASA Office of Planetary Protection." *NASA Office of Planetary Protection*. Web. 24 Aug. 2015. <http://planetaryprotection.nasa.gov/documents>.

"NSS Leads Formation of New Space Solar Power Organization." *NSS Leads Formation of New Space Solar Power Organization*. Web. 24 Aug. 2015. <http://www.nss.org/news/releases/pr20071010.html>.

"Non-Rocket Spacelaunch." *Wikipedia*. Wikimedia Foundation. Web. 24 Aug. 2015. <https://en.wikipedia.org/wiki/Non-rocket_spacelaunch>.

"OTRAG." *Wikipedia*. Wikimedia Foundation. Web. 24 Aug. 2015. <https://en.wikipedia.org/wiki/OTRAG>.

"Opportunity Rover." *Wikipedia*. Wikimedia Foundation. Web. 24 Aug. 2015. <https://en.wikipedia.org/wiki/Opportunity_(rover)>.

"Our Engine." *Our Engine*. Ad Astra. Web. 24 Aug. 2015. <http://www.adastrarocket.com/aarc/VASIMR>.

"Outer Space Treaty." *Wikipedia*. Wikimedia Foundation. Web. 24 Aug. 2015. <https://en.wikipedia.org/wiki/Outer_Space_Treaty>.

"Planetary Resources | The Asteroid Mining Company." *Planetary Resources Home Comments*. Web. 24 Aug. 2015. <http://www.planetaryresources.com/>.

"Plasma Window." *Wikipedia*. Wikimedia Foundation. Web. 24 Aug. 2015. <https://en.wikipedia.org/wiki/Plasma_window>.

"Prometheus (2012 Film)." *Wikipedia*. Wikimedia
Foundation. Web. 24 Aug. 2015.
<https://en.wikipedia.org/wiki/Prometheus_(2012_film
)>.

"Psychological and Sociological Effects of
Spaceflight." *Wikipedia*. Wikimedia Foundation. Web.
24 Aug. 2015.
<https://en.wikipedia.org/wiki/Psychological_and_soc
iological_effects_of_spaceflight#Psychosocial_and_Ps
ychiatric_Issues_during_an_Expedition_to_Mars>.

"Reaction Engines Ltd - Space Access: SKYLON."
Reaction Engines Ltd - Space Access: SKYLON. Web. 24
Aug. 2015.
<http://www.reactionengines.co.uk/space_skylon.html>

"Reusability: The Key to Making Human Life Multi-
Planetary." *SpaceX*. Web. 24 Aug. 2015.
<http://www.spacex.com/news/2013/03/31/reusability-
key-making-human-life-multi-planetary>.

Rice, Doyle, and William Welch. "Unmanned Antares
Rocket Explodes on Launch." *USA Today*. Gannett, 29
Oct. 2014. Web. 24 Aug. 2015.
<http://www.usatoday.com/story/tech/2014/10/28/nasa-
rocket-explodes-wallops-island/18080871/>.

"Robonaut 2 Technology Suite Offers Opportunities in
Vast Range of Industries." *Robonaut: Home*. Web. 24
Aug. 2015.
<http://robonaut.jsc.nasa.gov/default.asp>.
"Roundup Ready Crops." *The Roundup Ready
Controversy*. Web. 24 Aug. 2015.
<http://web.mit.edu/demoscience/Monsanto/about.html>

"Science Sample Return Vehicle for International
Space Station National Laboratory | Intuitive
Machines." *Science Sample Return Vehicle for
International Space Station National Laboratory |
Intuitive Machines*. Web. 24 Aug. 2015.
<https://intuitivemachines.com/news/trv/>.

"Seasteading." *Wikipedia*. Wikimedia Foundation. Web.
24 Aug. 2015.
<https://en.wikipedia.org/wiki/Seasteading>.

"Soylent - Free Your Body." *Soylent.com*. Web. 24
Aug. 2015. <https://www.soylent.com/>.

"Soylent - Free Your Body." *Soylent.com*. Web. 24
Aug. 2015. <https://www.soylent.com/>.

"Space Elevator Safety." *Wikipedia*. Wikimedia
Foundation. Web. 24 Aug. 2015.
<https://en.wikipedia.org/wiki/Space_elevator_safety

"Space Launch Vehicles." Web. 24 Aug. 2015.
<http://www.uh.edu/sicsa/library/media/publications/
AIAA_2013>.

"Space Mining: NASA And Caterpillar (CAT) Team Up To
Harness The Potential Of Mining On Asteroids, The
Moon And Mars." *International Business Times*. 8 Jan.
2014. Web. 19 Nov. 2014.

"Space Shuttle Columbia." *Wikipedia*. Wikimedia
Foundation. Web. 24 Aug. 2015.
<https://en.wikipedia.org/wiki/Space_Shuttle_Columbi
a_disaster>.

"Space Solar Power Exploratory Research and
Technology Program." *Wikipedia*. Wikimedia
Foundation. Web. 24 Aug. 2015.
<https://en.wikipedia.org/wiki/Space_Solar_Power_Exp
loratory_Research_and_Technology_program>.

"Space Tugboat Could Help Move Inexpensive Payloads
in Orbit." *Wired.com*. Conde Nast Digital. Web. 24
Aug. 2015. <http://www.wired.com/2012/05/space-
tugboat/>.

"Space-based Solar Power." *Wikipedia*. Wikimedia
Foundation. Web. 24 Aug. 2015.

<https://en.wikipedia.org/wiki/Space-based_solar_power>.

"Space-based Solar Power." *Wikipedia*. Wikimedia Foundation. Web. 24 Aug. 2015. <https://en.wikipedia.org/wiki/Space-based_solar_power>.

"SpaceX." *SpaceX*. Web. 24 Aug. 2015. <http://www.spacex.com/>.

"SpaceX Reusable Launch System Development Program." *Wikipedia*. Wikimedia Foundation. Web. 24 Aug. 2015. <https://en.wikipedia.org/wiki/SpaceX_reusable_launch_system_development_program>.

Spaleta, Steve. "SpaceX Falcon 9 Landing Test Captured By On-Board Cam | Video | Space.com." Web. 24 Aug. 2015. <http://www.space.com/26609-spacex-falcon-9-1st-stage-landing-captured-by-on-board-cam-video.html>.

"Step into the Rift." *Oculus*. Web. 24 Aug. 2015. <https://www.oculus.com/en-us/>.

"Strategic Defense Initiative." *Wikipedia*. Wikimedia Foundation. Web. 24 Aug. 2015. <https://en.wikipedia.org/wiki/Brilliant_Pebbles#Brilliant_Pebbles>.

"THE FIRSTPRIVATE SPACE HABITATIS HERE." *Bigelow Aerospace*. Web. 24 Aug. 2015. <http://bigelowaerospace.com/b330/>.

Tate, Karl. "How to Catch an Asteroid: NASA Mission Explained (Infographic) | Space.com." Web. 24 Aug. 2015. <http://www.space.com/20610-nasa-asteroid-capture-mission-infographic.html>.

"Terraforming." *Wikipedia*. Wikimedia Foundation. Web. 24 Aug. 2015. <https://en.wikipedia.org/wiki/Terraforming>.

"The Business Of Football." *Forbes*. Forbes Magazine. Web. 24 Aug. 2015. <http://www.forbes.com/nfl-valuations/list/>.

"The Economic Viability of Mars Colonization." *The Economic Viability of Mars Colonization*. Web. 24 Aug. 2015. <http://www.aleph.se/Trans/Tech/Space/mars.html>.

"The Seasteading Institute." *Seasteading Book - Beta*. Web. 24 Aug. 2015. <http://www.seasteading.org/book/seasteading-book-beta/>.

"The Seasteading Institute | Opening Humanity's next Frontier." *The Seasteading Institute*. Web. 24 Aug. 2015. <http://www.seasteading.org/>.

"The Space Elevator." Web. 24 Aug. 2015. <http://www.niac.usra.edu/files/studies/final_report/472Edwards.pdf>.

"The SpaceX Falcon Heavy Booster: Why Is It Important?" *The SpaceX Falcon Heavy Booster: Why Is It Important?* Web. 24 Aug. 2015. <http://www.nss.org/articles/falconheavy.html>.

"Thermal Radiation." *Wikipedia*. Wikimedia Foundation. Web. 22 June 2015. <https://en.wikipedia.org/wiki/Thermal_radiation>.

"UP Aerospace Inc. - Services." *UP Aerospace Inc. - Services*. Web. 24 Aug. 2015. <http://www.upaerospace.us.com/Services.html>.

"Virgin Galactic Spacecraft Crash Kills Pilot - BBC News." *BBC News*. Web. 24 Aug. 2015. <http://www.bbc.com/news/world-us-canada-29857182>.

"Virgin Galactic, the World's First Commercial Spaceline." *Virgin Galactic*. Web. 24 Aug. 2015. <http://www.virgingalactic.com/>.

"Voyager - The Interstellar Mission." *Voyager - The Interstellar Mission*. Web. 24 Aug. 2015. <http://voyager.jpl.nasa.gov/>.

Wall, Mike. "Deflecting Killer Asteroids Away From Earth: How We Could Do It | Asteroid 2005 YU55, Asteroids & Near-Earth Objects | Asteroid Impact & Mass Extinction | Space.com." Web. 24 Aug. 2015. <http://www.space.com/13524-deflecting-killer-asteroids-earth-impact-methods.html>.

"Welcome to Deep Space Industries | Deep Space Industries." *Deep Space Industries*. Web. 24 Aug. 2015. <http://deepspaceindustries.com/>.

"Why Elon Musk Wants to Launch a Space-Based Internet Service | MIT Technology Review." *MIT Technology Review*. 27 Jan. 2015. Web. 24 Aug. 2015. <http://www.technologyreview.com/news/534361/why-the-time-seems-right-for-a-space-based-internet-service/>.

"XCOR - Life-changing." *XCOR - Life-changing*. Web. 24 Aug. 2015. <http://www.xcor.com/error/>.

By Jeremy Hsu, SPACE.com Senior Writer. "New Private Spacesuit Unveiled With New York Flair | Space.com." Web. 24 Aug. 2015. <http://www.space.com/8782-private-spacesuit-unveiled-york-flair.html>.

"Kevlar Price." *Kevlar Price, Kevlar Price Suppliers and Manufacturers at Alibaba.com*. Web. 24 Aug. 2015. <http://www.alibaba.com/showroom/kevlar-price.html>.

www.ingramcontent.com/pod-product-compliance
Lightning Source LLC
Chambersburg PA
CBHW070807180526
45168CB00002B/523